The Writing School at Christ's Hospital: a hand-coloured aquatint taken from 'The History of Christ's Hospital' published by R. Ackermann in 1816.   E. 989-1965

English Handwriting
1540-1853

An illustrated survey based on material in the National Art Library, Victoria and Albert Museum

By JOYCE IRENE WHALLEY

LONDON: HER MAJESTY'S STATIONERY OFFICE 1969

Designed by HMSO/Alan Stephens
Printed in England for Her Majesty's Stationery Office
by Jarrold and Sons Ltd, Norwich

SBN 11 290047 X*

143,706

17/415

The Museum Library possesses a large collection of examples of lettering and penmanship ranging from illuminated manuscripts to engraved writing books and single specimens of fine calligraphy. The Italian section has long been known to students through the writings of the late James Wardrop (d.1957), formerly Deputy Keeper of the Library, who made a special study of the humanistic scripts of the Italian Renaissance; his zeal and knowledge were responsible for many acquisitions. English calligraphy was less well represented until the gifts and bequests of Sir Ambrose Heal (d.1959) and Sir Sidney Cockerell (d.1962) substantially augmented the collection already in the Library. Part of this material was shown in the exhibition 'Four Hundred Years of English Handwriting (1543–1943)', held at the Museum in 1964. The present monograph, by Miss Joyce Irene Whalley, Senior Research Assistant in the Library, presents, in permanent form, a comprehensive study of English calligraphic works in the Museum collection.

JOHN POPE-HENNESSY
Director

CONTENTS

ENDPAPERS

The alphabet and enlarged details on the endpapers are taken from
The Pen-mans Paradis, both pleasant & profitable by John Seddon, 1695.

In compiling this survey of English handwriting over a period of three hundred years, two limitations have been observed. No attempt has been made to deal with the actual technique of writing, except incidentally. Most of the published works considered here give a certain amount of detailed information on this subject, though in the case of some of the older books this is the part which has not survived. Writing technique is a highly specialised subject, moreover, with its own literature, which is to be found listed in the Subject Index of the National Art Library.

The second limitation observed in this survey has been that of the National Art Library itself. The Library's collection, built up over the last hundred years and particularly enriched by the generosity of the late Sir Ambrose Heal, is by no means representative of all periods or calligraphers. This has inevitably revealed itself in the choice of examples, since it was considered desirable to confine the survey to material actually available in the Library. A short-title catalogue of English writing-books and calligraphic manuscripts in the National Art Library is included with this survey.

The writing-books and manuscripts vary considerably in size. For the most part, no attempt has been made to reproduce all of the items in their actual size, but the clarity and legibility of the examples has been the paramount consideration. Finally, the opportunity has been taken to link the engraved copy-books with other contemporary calligraphic examples, and to place English handwriting in relation to the stylistic trends of the period under consideration.

Before the invention of printing in the mid-15th century, the traditional methods of recording information were by inscriptions cut in stone, clay, metal or wood, or by writing with quill or brush on papyrus, vellum or paper. In medieval Europe the most common method of communication was by handwritten vellum or paper documents. The number of people able to read and write at this time was limited, and almost entirely confined to the clergy – indeed any person who could write was usually a 'clericus', whence our word 'clerk', which perpetuates this original meaning. Since few rulers or their subjects could read or write with fluency, most high offices at court were held by ecclesiastics. But as political stability increased, and settled town life became more complicated, certain professions, such as the legal and medical, began to develop outside the clerical class. With the growth of trade, more and more people needed to communicate with one another and a separate body of professional scribes grew up. Nevertheless, throughout this period the art of writing remained an acquirement limited to comparatively few practitioners, and this in turn affected the form of the writing itself. An esoteric and highly contracted style was developed, easily understood by the initiated but remaining something of a mystery to the rest of the world. The professional scribe saved both time and labour by the use of contractions and abbreviations, while the scarcity (and therefore the cost) of parchment and paper also encouraged this custom. Not only did national hands develop, but also particular hands for different kinds of documents. The Papal Chancery, in its position as both a spiritual and a temporal power which employed a large number of scribes, played an important part in the development of cursive writing, and the universities, which had begun as training-grounds for the clergy, were also affected by the gradual secularisation of education.

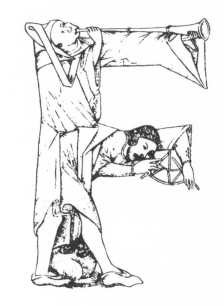

In England in the 15th century, in spite of the long-drawn-out civil wars, trade continued to increase and with it the importance of the middle class. We are fortunate in possessing letters written by members of the 'non-professional' writing public, such as the Paston family. This East Anglian family, involved in the various aspects of the wool trade, found the need, as many others like them must have done, to be constantly corresponding with their agents, lawyers, or members of their family – with the head of the house in London, with a son at the university, with husband, mother or friend. These people did not wish for the services of the professional scribe, preferring to write in their own hand and after their own fashion. With such ordinary, middle-class people the story of informal writing really begins.

England in the 16th century saw continuous development of centralised and stable government—conditions which enabled trade to prosper and the wealth and importance of the middle-class to increase. Moreover, soon after the beginning of the century the new arts of printing and engraving became established in England resulting in a multiplication of books which assisted the spread of learning, and increased the desire for education in the twin arts of reading and writing. The

dissolution of the monasteries under Henry VIII not only scattered the monks with their learning, but also dispersed the monastic libraries. In addition to the various internal influences which provided a suitable soil for new ideas, by the middle of the century Italian humanist scholarship was also becoming known to an increasing number of people, both in the universities and at court. Roger Ascham, for example, who was employed to teach the children of Henry VIII, was not only familiar with contemporary Italian scholarship, but also wrote a fine italic hand. This hand, as recent studies have shown, was widely written by people of education in England, including members of the royal family. Even if the main body of a letter might be written in the everyday hand known as 'secretary' (see Glossary), the signature at least might well be in a fine italic. But, in spite of the increase in writing and the obvious need for instruction, it is not until the second half of the 16th century that the first published English writing-book appeared. This was 'A booke containing divers sortes of hands' by John de Beauchesne and John Baildon, published in London in 1570.

During the 17th century, although England was again troubled by civil war, certain aspects of everyday life continued much as before. There was a further slow spread of literacy and a continuous development of trade, which, together with the scattering of families consequent upon the Civil War, all led to even greater need for written communication. And it is in the early part of this century that there thus arose a new profession in England, that of the writing-master. The writing-master's position in society was always somewhat anomalous – was he a member of the learned professions or not? He thought he was – where would they be without him? The learned professions and the scholars on their part tended to despise the 'mere scrivener', and it is amusing for us to trace the result of this struggle for an accepted position in society in the works of the writing-masters themselves. The position was not helped by the fact that most of the grammar schools expected their pupils to be able to write adequately before their arrival at such institutions. However, in many cases some small provision was made for writing lessons – but after school hours or on the half-holiday! Although each schoolmaster might be expected to be able to give some instruction in the art of writing, there was also a class of itinerant writing-masters who went about the country offering their services to schools and individuals. And although no doubt many of these were quite competent, it did nothing to raise the standing of the profession, when the art of writing might be peddled in the same way as ribbons and laces. Hence the writing-master, in his published works, liked to sprinkle his examples with Latin texts or quotations from the classics, and generally to show an acquaintance with foreign learning. In addition, wherever possible, he tried to consolidate his standing by obtaining a flattering foreword, or perhaps a poem, from a well-known scholar – or at least from a friend.

But the need to show a wide range of scripts and a learned background was more typical of the

17th century than the 18th, for although this practice continued to some extent, it was less necessary. In the 17th century there were still special court or legal hands for the various types of legal documents. The writing-master was expected to demonstrate his skill in all varieties of script, during this time when writing was still an art with a limited public. But by the early 18th century the conflict between the different writing styles was almost over, and it was clear as the century progressed that the needs of commerce were uppermost. The artistic flourishes of a calligraphy likely to appeal to a leisured class gave way to an unashamed practical approach. A good clear round hand and a knowledge of book-keeping, with a grounding in basic letter-forms when young, were now the main requirements, and writing-masters felt themselves to be an established class, no longer needing to attach themselves to one of the other learned professions. Their numbers multiplied as British trade and commerce expanded. There was more and more need for clerks who could be quickly taught, and then relied on to perform with speed and clarity the various functions of business life. These needs are reflected in the titles of the copy-books of the period: 'The Young Merchant's Assistant', 'The British Youth's Instructor; or, the Useful Penman', and they offer 'various examples adapted to form the man of business'. And to show that the profession had fully arrived, in 1763 came William Massey's 'The origin and progress of letters', which contained as a second part 'A compendious account of the most celebrated English penmen, with the titles and characters of the books they have published both from the rolling and letter press' – the first, and for a long time the only, book on the subject of the English writing-masters.

The middle of the 18th century was perhaps the peak period of English handwriting until (at least in some quarters) it again reached a high standard in recent years. The supremacy of the English hand, neat, clear, quick and practical, became as generally accepted as it was widely known – a position brought about by the ubiquity of English bills of lading and letters of credit. Thereafter there was little development, only perhaps a weakening or mannerism, as in some hands the 'thicks' and 'thins' were emphasised at the expense of legibility. The steel pen began slowly to replace the quill and writing became an accepted part of the ordinary school curriculum. The writing-school at Christ's Hospital was particularly famous and was portrayed in an aquatint in Ackermann's 'History of Christ's Hospital', 1816 (frontispiece). The general increase in literacy was hastened in the 1840s by the new educational acts, which were to extend the same plain, rather dull handwriting to a far wider field. It is appropriate to terminate this survey at the period when either through formal education or by means of books of self-help, the knowledge (if not the art) of writing was being spread through all the country. Not until the end of the 19th century did anyone begin again to give serious consideration as to the style of handwriting that was then being perpetrated in educational establishments. But from that point a new story began which leads us into the twentieth century and to the present revival of interest in the art of fine writing. Examples of this modern calligraphy are also to be found in the Library's collection, beginning with the influential work of William Morris and Edward Johnston and continuing to the present decade, and covering the period when English handwriting has again reached a significant position.

An enlarged detail from *The Pens Transcendencie; or, faire writings labyrinth* by Edward Cocker, 1657.

The decorated initials on pages ix–xi are taken from the Banderolles/Garnier Manuscript (see page xiii).

The earliest English writing-book in the Library is a manuscript dating from about 1540 and consisting of several sets of elaborate initials, two of which have been identified as being copies after 'the Master of the Banderolles' and Noël Garnier (plates 1–4). The other models have not yet been identified. Beside the elaborate initials of Noël Garnier, the English scribe has written a variety of copies, mostly in the secretary hand. This manuscript was perhaps a scribe's sample book, to show what he could do, or it may have been a pupil's copy-book. Evidence on the fly-leaf (plate 4) suggests that the manuscript was in the south of England fairly early in its career, and some interesting scribbles showing familiarity with different hands appear on the same page.

Another early calligraphic manuscript is a book of prayers, possibly written by Esther Inglis (1571–1624; plate 11a), one of the few well-known women calligraphers, or by one of her followers. This little book of devotions contains a considerable variety of contemporary hands, and in this respect is in line with the subsequent development of the copy-book proper. Apart from the work of professional calligraphers, the Library also possesses examples of writing of a non-professional kind. One such is a letter from Queen Elizabeth (plate 7), written in a secretary hand by an official, and signed by her in italic, the hand often used for the more important parts of a letter, or for quotations. There are also many other letters and notebooks of the 16th and 17th centuries in the Library, which reveal a knowledge of writing among more classes of the population than had been the case in the previous century. When considering the calligraphy of this period, the use made of fine hands as a form of decoration also should be noted. The miniatures by Nicholas Hilliard (plates 5 and 6), for example, reveal many examples of fine calligraphic inscriptions incorporated as a part of the composition. Hilliard's training as a goldsmith points to another field where the graver took over from the pen, namely in inscriptions on gold and silver plate. In the monumental arts, however, it was lettering rather than calligraphy which provided the model.

The manuscript copy-book was obviously limited in its influence, even though written in the master's own hand. The way to reach a wider public was to publish a book of copies, engraved either on wood or copper. This method had its obvious disadvantages, and there were continual arguments about its usefulness – whether the multiplicity of copies did not cheapen the master's wares; whether the hand of the engraver would 'interpret' rather than copy the letters in front of him. Some writing-masters gave high praise to their engravers; some masters, like Edward Cocker (plates 23–28), preferred to do all the work themselves. Others refer fretfully to 'botchers' who ruin the beauty of the master-copy. But of the usefulness of the published work in spreading the fame of the writer there was no doubt; moreover, with very little effort (or scrupulousness) the same plate could be re-used many times. With no change perhaps save that

of a title-page, another book was ready to bring in more money and pupils.

The earliest English published book of copies in the Library is 'The Pens Excellencie; or, the Secretaries Delighte', by Martin Billingsley (plates 13, 15, 16). Possibly first published in 1616, the Museum copy is dated 1618. Billingsley was writing-master to Charles I when Prince of Wales, and specimens of the King's writing in later life are in the Forster Collection (plate 14). Billingsley prefaces his examples of the various hands with some pages of text, in which he not only explains the method of forming the different letters, but also makes some interesting comments on the subject of writing in general. As he is the first of the writing-masters to be considered here, it is worth examining his remarks in some detail. It must be remembered that informal cursive writing was to some extent a new art, and the writing-master still needed to 'sell' his wares, also that his public was limited and mainly upper class. But already Billingsley can perceive a use for writing even among those who may need no more than the ability to keep simple trade accounts.

'It is necessary for all (you know) to write; and those that cannot finde what a multitude of inconveniences doe come upon them for want of it.' Billingsley continues, 'There are those that thinke writing to be onely a hand-labour, and so they can write to keepe a dirty shop-booke they care for no more.' But its excellencies are above this: it is 'the key which opens a passage to the descrying and finding out of innumerable treasures; the handmaid to memory: the register and recorder of all the arts: and the very mouth whereby a man familiarly confereth with his friend, though the distance of thousands of miles be betwixt them.'

Billingsley also had his eye on another possible source of pupils: 'And herein (by the way) suffer me not to give connivance to that ungrounded opinion of many, who affirm writing to be altogether unnecessary for women. . . . If any art be commendable in a woman . . . it is this of writing, whereby they, commonly having not the best memories (especially concerning matters of moment), may commit many worthy and excellent things to writing, which may occasionally minister unto them matters of much solace.' But Billingsley does not expect too much from his female pupils. The roman hand, he says, 'is conceived to be the easiest that is written with the pen, and to be taught in the shortest time: Therefore it is usually taught to women, for as much as they (having not the patience to take any great paines, besides phantasticall and humorsome), must be taught that which they may easily learne, otherwise they are uncertaine of their proceedings, because their minds are (upon light occasion) easily drawne from the first resolution.'

Billingsley also expresses himself on another subject which was to come up again and again over the years, until buried by the overriding needs of trade and commerce: 'Lastly, to use any strange, borrowed or inforc'd tricks and knots in or about writing other then with the celerity of the hand are to be performed, is rather to set an inglorious glosse upon a simple peece of worke, then to give a comely lustre to a perfect patterne; they being as unnaturall to writing as a surfet is to a temperate mans body.'

This austere advice, to be echoed frequently by later writing-masters of the same way of thought, was certainly not to the liking of Edward Cocker (1631–76), one of the most engaging practitioners of the art, whose vast output dominated the middle and later years of the century.

The Library has no specimen of Cocker's work dating before 1657, on the eve of the Restoration. But from this year until 1703 there are twenty-nine copies of his publications. Many show signs of being nothing but a rehash of earlier works, but the titles are always new and splendid: 'Arts Glory; or, the pen-man's treasurie', 'Penna Volans; or, the young mans accomplishment', 'Multum in Parvo; or, the pen's gallantrie', 'The Pens Transcendency; or, fair writings store-house'.

Ready to push the virtues of his art, take on a critic, or explain the complexities of a letter-form with equal exuberance, Cocker was a competent engraver of his own works as well as a versatile calligrapher, adorning his pages with labyrinthine 'strikings' to form a variety of shapes, and hurling a defiant verse at those who said such things had nothing to do with the art of fair writing:

'Some sordid sotts
Cry downe rare knotts,
But art shall shine
And envie pine
And still my pen shall flourish.'

His calligraphic intricacies form a fitting complement to the ornate, decorative style of the Restoration period, with its elaborateness and over-adornment, be it in costume or the applied arts – indeed the decoration on Susan Meadows's writing-desk (plate 24) might well have been taken from one of Cocker's own calligraphic designs with which it is exactly contemporary, and the same may be said of the goldsmiths' work of the period.

In common with his fellow writing-masters, Edward Cocker had an exalted opinion of his chosen profession: 'Writing is an art neither mechanical nor liberal, yet the parent and original of both. Not a science, yet the way to all sciences. Not a virtue, yet the dispenser and herald of virtues; serving naturally for the illustration of the mind and the delight of the eyes. . . . This commendable art . . . the furtherance of commerce, the strength of societies, the sweet entercourse of friends absent, the progress of fame . . . the tie of civil life, the bond of the weal publique.' As the practitioner of so high an art, the writing-master considered himself the equal of the greatest scholar, and proved his point further by giving his examples for copying in Latin, French and other languages, and by showing an apparent familiarity with the classics and the Bible. And if this should not be sufficient, the writing-master's friends might be depended upon to add their recommendation:

'On this admired book and its more admirable author:

Each Draught With Admirable Rarities Done   (EDWARD)
Choice Ovall-Circling-Knots Exactly Run.'   (COCKER)

and from his publisher and bookseller:

'Multum in Parvo' I have thousands sold
Whose plates with often printing are grown old
'Magnum in Parvo' here you now behold
Ingrav'd in silver but deserving gold.'

But perhaps a less partial comment comes from Samuel Pepys, who employed Cocker to engrave some tables on a slide-rule; having watched him work and talked with him, he commented in his diary, 'Well pleased with his company and better with his judgement.'

In addition to engraved examples of every sort of current hand, and varieties of knots and cunning inventions, Cocker also provided for the student printed details of technique. For command of hand, he said, 'see that your ink be not too thick, that your paper be smoothe and free from wrinckle and hairs or anything, that you hold your pen steady and keep your paper from stirring'. Each individual hand and letter-form is carefully described, and his instructions are cheered on with little verses – on the Italian and roman hands he says:

'These practis'd well may mount us where proud Rome
Though hills were set on hills shall never come.'

After Edward Cocker there was never again quite the same exuberance, or the same style. There were others who also favoured the flourishes and the knots, though they tended to become more restrained, as in the work of John Seddon towards the end of the century (plate 41). Moreover, there had always been advocates of the unadorned hand, typified in the restrained and elegant examples of Peter Gery. It was this latter style which was to set the pattern for the future development of English handwriting, although that future too was not to be without controversies.

With Peter Gery (plates 29–32), indeed, we come up against one of the minor controversies of the writing scene – minor in that it did not affect the style of the writing, but of considerable importance nevertheless. This was the vexed question of the relation between the engraved and the handwritten version of the copy. In the introduction to Ayres's 'Tutor to Penmanship' the engraver, Sturt, comments on Gery's attitude to his engraver, saying that 'being a peevish man' he 'would not afford his engraver the help and directions necessary for such an undertaking'. We have noted that Edward Cocker usually engraved his own copy-books, and in the next century George Bickham was to show his skill almost equally as an engraver of writing-books, and as a practitioner. Richard Clark, in his preface to his 'Practical and ornamental Penmanship', 1758, records the actual method of transferring the original written copy to the engraved page. Clark also adds the comment that 'mankind in general' looks 'upon them [the engraved plates] as the sole production of the engraver, and not of the writing master. . . . All engraved writings are first designed and wrote by some master, or drawn in backwards by the engraver. . . . For as it is impracticable for the engraver to produce an elegant piece of engraved writing, without the assistance of the master in forming the design for him, so it is likewise impossible for the penman to multiply his performances, and transmit his works to posterity without the aid of the able and judicious engraver.' This is a fair opinion, and indeed the good engravers of writing-books in the 18th century were almost as famous as the writing-masters they served, and proudly signed their names on an equal footing. 'John Langton inv. et scr., George Bickham sculp.' we read (plate 61), and similar phrases appear on the plates of other well-known works.

After the comparatively mild recriminations over the engraving of copy-books we come to the great controversy over style at the turn of the century. At this period the introductory pages of the writing-books fairly bubble with charges and counter-charges: John Ayres (fl. 1680–1705), George Shelley (1666?–1736?), John Clark (1683–1736) and Charles Snell (1667–1733) were among the best-known writing-masters of their day, and each of them had something fiercely derogatory to say about the others of his profession. The main question, as we have indicated, was whether the master was justified in including 'owls, apes and monsters, and sprigg'd letters' in his copy-books, but the attack became personal: 'As for men of my own profession . . . I expect their censures, but value them not, since they are consequences naturally flowing from malice or invincible ignorance' wrote Charles Snell. John Ayres was not prepared to accept that. He advises those of Snell's 'own profession to be good natur'd and docible and lay by that malice and invincible ignorance he charges them wth, and if it be possible, conceive but as great an opinion of ye gentleman as he doth of himself.'

In his argument over ornament, Snell was on the winning side. In 'The Art of Writing' (plates 48–50), he says, 'I have here furnish'd youth with such plain, easie and useful examples in the several hands as may help fit them for business', and he goes on to affirm, 'That merchants and clerks, are so far from admitting those wild fancies, and the strokes they [his opponents] have so plentifully struck through the body of their writing, as a part of penmanship; that they

despise and scorn them.' 'Let your endeavours be to make your handwriting legible, expeditious and beautiful as you can; for these three qualities are what will render it the most useful'; he continues, 'the examples as anyone may see, were not designed for a gaudy show among knots'.

But John Clark also had his say. On the ornamental aspect of penmanship he wrote, 'This part has been exploded by some because not of immediate use in business, or rather thro' ignorance or want of capacity to do anything agreeable that way. . . . Let not your ornament obscure your writing, but let it be easy and natural'. Clark continued, 'The practice of striking and sprigging of letters are pretty ingenious exercises for youths at their leisure hours, and may also serve to please such as admire the fancy of the pen as well as the solid use of it'; and again, 'From hence appears the folly and ill-nature of a late author, in the violent noise he made about the sprigging of letters and the pencilling of flourishes; and the scurrilous treatment of all other penmen upon that score. . . .' But it was a lost cause, and at this distance of time and in the present state of handwriting and general indifference to it, we can only marvel at the passions that were roused over the subject of writing at all. George Bickham, in the most splendid writing-book published in England, may have the last word on the subject: 'Writing is the first step and the essential in furnishing out the man of business. . . . Plain, strong and neat writing as it best answers the designs for use and beauty; so it has most obtained among men of business.'

The work of the various members of the Bickham family extends over the middle years of the 18th century, and also covers a variety of different aspects of engraved writing. For the purposes of this study, the volume entitled 'The Universal Penman' (plates 57–60) is of the greatest importance. Published first in parts between 1733 and 1741, it is one of the most splendid of the English writing-books, and certainly one of the largest. It consists of 212 engraved folio plates, including a title-page, dedication, list of contents and an elaborate pictorial frontispiece 'The Representative'. For this undertaking, George Bickham had solicited examples of their work from no less than twenty-five contemporary penmen. A few examples appear to be from his own hand and many are certainly engraved by him. The book not only displays the great variety of the hands then current for all types of use and sets out various business forms, but also imparts advice both commercial and moral, 'the whole embellish'd with beautiful decorations for the amusement of the curious'. Indeed, the decorative head-pieces and genre scenes with which the work is lavishly adorned, combined with the general purpose of the work and the choice of examples, give an interesting picture of the 18th-century scene.

George Bickham was also responsible for other writing-books, though nothing on so grand a scale was ever again attempted; but he had also an extremely high reputation as an engraver of other people's work, and not only in the field of pure calligraphy. Other members of his family maintained the engraving tradition, and their work enables us briefly to consider other *fields in which the calligrapher was to prove important. In 'The British Monarchy' and in 'The Musical Entertainer', two other folio works associated with the Bickham family, we see their skill in the engraving of music and words of songs, in the lettering of maps, and in long descriptive pages of text produced by engraving instead of printing. These aspects of the engravers' art continued to show the influence of the contemporary writing-master into the 19th century, while many a printed book was likewise adorned with an additional title-page of calligraphic design.*

In the last part of the 18th century most writing-masters continued to display their versatility as heretofore, but the need for such variety was declining. Well into the 19th century pupils were still expected to be able to produce examples of a style of writing they were unlikely ever to require in daily life. A late 19th-century edition of Vere Foster's copy-book in the Library contains sets of ornamental hands in the manner of those of earlier centuries, which the pupil, who was to live into the 20th century, has copied with all the expertise of his 17th or 18th-century predecessor. But the writing of these elaborate hands had now become little more than a discipline, rather like Latin verbs for many a schoolboy, and this is reflected in the examples chosen for the last part of this study. Here the plain hand and the business text are supreme. Most copy-books continued to offer some examples of decorative and legal hands, but gradually these forms were taken more and more into the realm of type or wood engraving, and the days of the elaborate engraved copy-books were over. With the great increase in the number of schools, and need for teachers of handwriting for the masses, the status of the writing-master declined. When every man could write, the profession fell apart and the outstanding names of the 19th century are few compared with those of the 18th. It is a fitting comment to end this study with the selection from 'Cassell's Popular Educator' (plates 79 and 80), since this work, intended for self-teaching among those who had not received the benefit of a formal or an extended education, reduced the once-wide choice of hands to three simple basic styles. And in this state English handwriting remained until the close of the 19th century.

ENGLISH CALLIGRAPHIC MANUSCRIPTS IN THE NATIONAL ART LIBRARY, *c.*1540–*c.*1840

A writing-book containing five sets of decorative alphabets (some incomplete) of which one is after the Master of the Banderolles and another after Noël Garnier, together with numerous calligraphic specimens, presumably by an English scribe. *c.* 1540–*c.* 1567.

Summarie expositions upon sundrie notable sentences of the Olde Testament made in form of praiers [etc.]. Possibly written by Esther Inglis. Last quarter of the 16th century.

Three copy-sheets, the first line of each possibly written out by the master, and in two instances introduced by elaborate historiated initials. Two of the sheets are signed 'Thomas Carwytham'. *c.* 1600.

Anagram by J. Durant on the name of Nicholas Hilliard, written out by Peter Bales. *c.* 1610.

Examples of handwriting, mostly legal hands, and concerning transactions in Westmorland, Cumberland, Lancashire, Sussex [etc.]. Written out and signed by Richard Jackman. 1620.

A coppie booke of some severall hands used in 1677. Written out by Andrew Andrews. 1677.

Examples of handwriting, some possibly by William Raven and James Austen. 1688.

Two books of examples of handwriting, both signed by John Stonestreet. 1688?

Examples of handwriting, possibly by John Stonestreet, in red and black with elaborately decorated initial letters. *c.* 1690.

Child's exercise-book, containing examples of a variety of different hands. *c.* 1805?

Four folders, formerly in the possession of Sir Ambrose Heal, and containing miscellaneous material, mostly connected with handwriting. Nos. 3 and 4 contain 18th- and 19th-century manuscript material.

St. Valentine's Day greeting addressed to Master G. Hobart of Catton. 1811?

The 'Parch', a book of arithmetical exercises, drawings and examples of penmanship written out by Sir Henry Cole when a thirteen-year-old schoolboy at Christ's Hospital. 1821.

A copy-book signed 'Edward Daniel Riches', containing a variety of single-line copies written out by a teacher and pupil. First half of 19th century.

A copy-book written out and signed by William Coham Turner when a pupil at Bray's Academy, Barnstaple. 1834.

A copy-book written out and signed by William Coham Turner when a pupil at Bray's Academy, Barnstaple; it contains exercises dated between 20 August and 11 December 1835.

A school writing-book formerly belonging to H. C. Roper, containing poems and extracts from chemistry lectures. 1840–41.

SHORT-TITLE CATALOGUE OF ENGLISH WRITING-BOOKS PUBLISHED BEFORE 1800 IN THE NATIONAL ART LIBRARY

AYRES, John
A Tutor to Penmanship. (1698)

BANSON, William
The Merchants Penman. (1702)
BICKHAM, George [Junior?]
The Drawing and Writing Tutor. [*c.* 1730]
BICKHAM, George
Penmanship in its Utmost Beauty and Extent. 1731
The Universal Penman.
(1741, i.e. 1733–41)

Another ed. (1743)
Another ed. [*c.* 1745]
The United Pen-men for Forming the Man of Business. 1743
The British Youth's Instructor. 1754
The Whole System of Penmanship. 1754
BICKHAM, George and John
Universal Penmanship. [*c.* 1740]
BILLINGSLEY, Martin
The Pens Excellencie. (1618)

BOWLES, Carrington
Bowles's Young Lawyers Tutor. 1764
BROOKS, William
A Delightful Recreation for the Industrious. (1717)

CHAMPION, Joseph
Penmanship Illustrated. (1759)
The Penman's Employment. 1763
Bowles's New and Complete Alphabets. [*c.* 1770?]
New, and Complete

Alphabets. 1794
The Young Clerk, and
Tradesman's Directory. 1798
CHINNERY, William
Writing and Drawing made
Easy. (The Compendious
Emblematist.) 1750
    Another ed. [c. 1760]
     Another copy.
CLARK, John
The Penman's Diversion. (1710)
Writing Improv'd. (1714)
[i.e. c. 1727?]
CLARK, Richard
Practical and Ornamental
Penmanship. 1758
CLERK.
The Young Clerk's Assistant.
(1733)
COCKER, Edward
Arts Glory. 1657
    Another ed.
The Pens Transcendencie; or,
Faire Writings Labyrinth. (1657)
The Pens Triumph. 1658
    Another ed. 1659
Multum in Parvo. 1660
    Another ed. 1661
Penna Volans. 1661
    Another copy.
    Another ed. 1661
     Another copy.
The Guide to Penmanship. 1664
[i.e. c. 1670]
The Tutor to Writing and
Arithmetic. 1664
    Another ed.
The Young Clerk's Copy-book.
1664
The Pens Celerity. 1667
The Pens Transcendency; or, Fair
Writings Store-House. 1668
    Another ed.
Magnum in Parvo. 1672
    Another ed.
England's Pen-man. 1703
COOTE, Edward
The English School-Master. 1684
COPY-BOOK
A Coppie Booke. 1660
COPY-BOOK
An Arithmetical Copy-book.
[c. 1720]

DANIEL, Richard
Daniel's Copy Book. 1664
    Another ed. (1680)
DAVIES, John
The Writing Schoolemaster. 1648

ELDER, William
The Modish Penman. [c. 1691]

FURBOR, T.
Bowles's Penman's Delight. [1810?]

GERY, Peter
Gerii, Viri in Arte Scriptoria
Quondam Celeberrimi Opera; or,
a Copie Book of All the Hands
now in Use. [c. 1660]
GETHING, Richard
Calligraphotechnia. 1642
    Another ed. 1652
Chiro-graphia. 1645

LANGTON, John
A New Copy-book of the Italian-
hand. 1727
LLOYD, Edward
The Young Merchant's Assistant.
(1751)

McARTHUR, Samuel
A New Copy Book of Round
Text, Half Text and Small Hand.
[c. 1755]
MASSEY, William
The Origin and Progress of Letters.
1763
MILNS, William
The Penman's Repository. 1795
MORE, Robert
Of the First Invention of Writing.
(1716)

PENMAN
The Select Penman, Consisting
of Copious Extracts from All the
most Excellent Performances
now in Esteem. [c. 1755?]
PULMAN, Robert
Writing Illustrated. [1766?]
    Another copy.
Round Hand Copies and other
Pieces. (1779)

RICHARDS, William
The Compleat Penman. (1738)
    Another ed. bound in The
    Universal Library of Trade
    and Commerce. (1747)

SEDDON, John
The Pen-man's Paradis, both
Pleasant & Profitable. (1695)
The Ingenious Youth's
Companion. [c. 1705]
SERLE, Ambrose
A Treatise on the Art of Writing.
1766
SHELLEY, George
The Penman's Magazine. 1705
Natural Writing in all the Hands.
(1709)
Penna Volans. [c. 1710]
The Second Part of Natural
Writing. (1714)
SMITH, Duncan
The Academical Instructor. 1794
SNELL, Charles
The Penman's Treasury Open'd.
(1694)
The Art of Writing in its Theory
and Practice. 1712 [i.e. 1739]

TOMKINS, Thomas
The Beauties of Writing
Exemplified in a Variety of Plain
and Ornamental Penmanship. 1777

VARIETY
Variety: a New Copy Book.
[c. 1760]

WATSON, Thomas
A Copy Book Enriched with
Great Variety of the most Useful
& Modish Hands. [c. 1690]
WEBB, Joseph
Webb's Useful Penmanship. 1796
WESTON, Thomas
A Copy-book Written for the Use
of the Young-gentlemen at the
Academy in Greenwich. 1726
WIGAN, Eleazer
Practical Arithmetic: an
Introduction to ye whole Art,
wherein the most Necessary Rules
are Fairly Describ'd in the Usuall
Hands. (1694) [1696?]

FURTHER READING

MASSEY, William. The origin and progress of letters. An essay, in two parts. . . . The second part consists of a compendious account of the most celebrated English penmen [etc.]. 1763
This book, now over two hundred years old, is still of the greatest importance for anyone interested in early calligraphy and the English writing-masters. The fact that it deals with many calligraphers who were contemporaries or near-contemporaries of the author gives it a special significance.

HEAL, Sir Ambrose: The English writing-masters and their copy books, 1570–1800. 1931
This book is still the only book dealing fully with the subject. It is divided into two parts, the first giving biographical details of the writing-masters, the second part containing bibliographical lists of their works. Since Heal's book was written, a certain amount of new material has come to light, but until a new edition of this work appears, it remains the most important, and indeed the only large-scale, study of the subject. Sir Ambrose Heal was a great benefactor of the National Art Library, and many of the books mentioned as in his collection are now in fact part of the Library. 'The English writing-masters' contains an introduction by Stanley Morison on the development of handwriting.

Many books on the technique of handwriting include a brief survey of the historical background and place the English styles in a European context. Alfred Fairbank's 'A Book of Scripts', is a useful non-technical survey of the subject which gives examples of both English and Continental hands.

There are also some detailed studies of limited periods of English handwriting, aimed more at the specialist than the general reader. Two of these are:

SCHULZ, Herbert C. The teaching of handwriting in Tudor and Stuart times. In *The Huntington Library Quarterly*, no. 4, 1943.

FAIRBANK, Alfred John, and WOLPE, Berthold: Renaissance handwriting: an anthology. 1960.

LIST OF PLATES

Frontispiece: Writing school at Christ's Hospital, by Rudolph Ackermann

1, 2, 3, 4   16th-century 'Banderolles/Garnier' manuscript copy-book

5a, 5b, 6a   Portrait miniatures by Nicholas Hilliard

6b   Signature of Nicholas Hilliard

7   Letter of Queen Elizabeth

8   Copy-sheet by Thomas Carwytham

9   Letter from Lord Burghley

10a   Manuscript poem

10b   Fruit trencher

11a   Manuscript possibly by Esther Inglis

11b   Set of fruit trenchers

12   Orb and cross in manuscript

13   *The Pens Excellencie*

14   Letter from Charles I

15a, 15b, 16a, 16b   *The Pens Excellencie*

17, 18   *Calligraphotechnia*

19, 20   *Chiro-graphia*

21, 22a, 22b   *The Writing Schoole-master*

23   *The Pens Transcendencie; or, faire writings labyrinth*

24   Susan Meadow's writing-desk

25   Portrait of Edward Cocker

26   *Penna Volans*

27   *The Pens Transcendency; or, fair writings store-house*

28   *Magnum in Parvo*

29, 30, 31, 32   *Gerii, Viri in Arte Scriptoria Quondam Celeberrimi Opera*

33   Manuscript, possibly by John Stonestreet

34a   *The Modish Penman*

34b   Indicating lock of cast brass

35, 36   *A Copy-book Enriched with Great Variety*

37   *A Tutor to Penmanship*

38   Two-handled silver cup

39   Manuscript bill

40   Letter written by John Watts

41   *The Pen-man's Paradis*

42   Portrait of George Shelley

43, 44, 45, 46   *Natural Writing in all the Hands*

47   *Penna Volans*

48, 49, 50   *The Art of Writing*

51, 52, 53   *A Delightful Recreation for the Industrious*

54   Silver box with inscription

55, 56   *A Copy-book Written for the Use of the Young-Gentlemen at the Academy in Greenwich*

57, 58, 59, 60   *The Universal Penman*

61   *A New Copy-book of the Italian-Hand*

62   *Writing and Drawing made Easy. (The Compendious Emblematist)*

63   *The Young Merchant's Assistant*

64   Manuscript bill with engraved bill-head

65, 66   *A New Copy Book of Round Text, Half Text and Small Hand*

67, 68   *The Penman's Employment*

69   *The Beauties of Writing*

70   Portrait of Thomas Tomkins

71   *The Academical Instructor*

72, 73   *Webb's Useful Penmanship*

74, 75, 76   Manuscript copy-book written by William Turner

77, 78   Manuscript copy-book written by Edward Riches

79, 80   *Cassell's Popular Educator*

81   Hand with quill-pen, from *The Writing Schoolemaster*

82   Seventeenth-century instructions on writing

83   Silver inkstand

84a   Seventeenth-century receipt for ink

84b   Writing-ink street-cry

85   Eighteenth-century 'Directions for Learners'

86   Silver inkstand by Paul de Lamerie

87a   Portable writing-box

87b   Ivory pen-knife

88   Porcelain inkstand

89   Hand with steel pen, from *The Popular Educator*

90   Writing class from *A Manual of Writing*, by M. A. Mulhauser

xxiii

Manuscript

*This manuscript, written on vellum, contains five sets of
decorative alphabets, two of which have been identified as
being after the 'Master of the Banderolles' (not shown)
and Noël Garnier (plates 1, 2 and 3, upper register).
The various texts, written at the side of the capital letters,
are by an English scribe, and the manuscript was probably
his sample book. Dates between 1543 and 1567 appear in
the work, which was in the south of England early in
its existence and may have been written there. Richard
Jones (or Johns), whose name appears on one of the pages,
has not been identified. This example (f. 8v) shows the
letter 'A'.*

12 × 9 inches

L 2090–1937

Manuscript

Further examples of scripts from the 16th-century 'Banderolles/Garnier' manuscript, showing both continuous examples of writing and individual letters. This example (f.11r) shows the letter 'F'.

12×9 inches

L 2090–1937

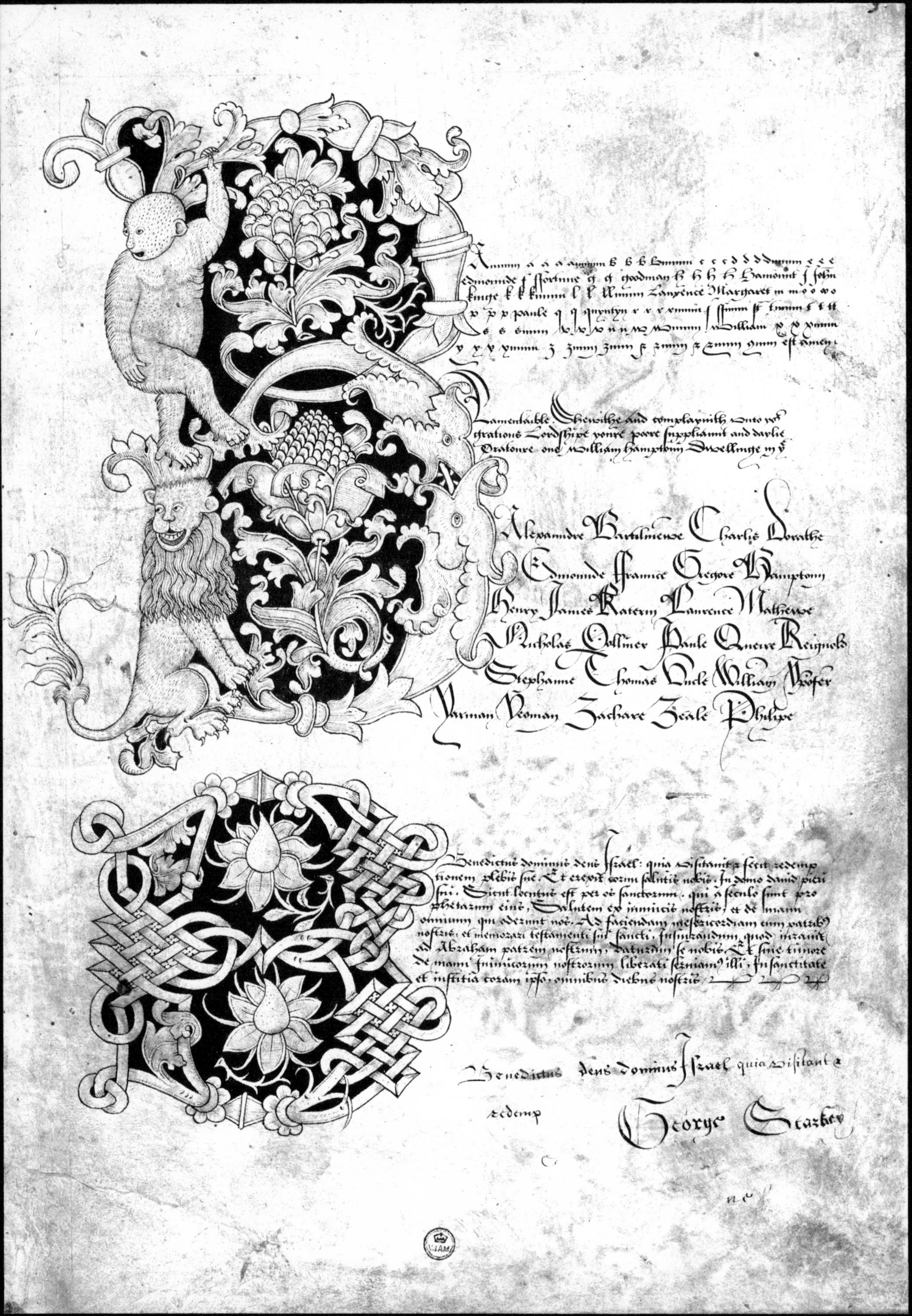

3

Manuscript

This leaf from the 16th-century 'Banderolles/Garnier' manuscript (f. 9r, the letter 'B'), not only shows examples of writing in English and Latin but another hand – perhaps that of George Starkey? – has given his version in a scribble at the bottom of the page.

12 × 9 inches

L 2090–1937

4 (right)

Manuscript

This enlarged detail from a blank leaf (f. 28v) of the 16th-century 'Banderolles/Garnier' manuscript, shows a variety of scribbles of about the same date as the work itself. They are interesting for the personal names and place-names they include as well as for the different styles of writing they show – possibly they are by the same idle scribbler who has been at work on other pages of the manuscript.

12 × 9 inches

L 2090–1937

memo memorandum

Robert Jones I pray

trustie and welbeloved frende

This Indenture made the
first day of Auguste 1552

primo Edward of ego Hugo ap

omnes hum
om
Thomas
James Edmunton

James monnyngtonne

James monnyngtonne

richmou

omnibus emma

memorandum

hamptonne

Rychmounde

Sense

6a (above)

Another enlarged portrait miniature of an unknown man by Nicholas Hilliard, dated 1588, with a fine italic inscription showing stylistic affinities with the painting it so fittingly complements.

$2\frac{3}{8} \times 2$ inches

P 21–1942

6b (below)

This example of the signature of the miniature-painter Nicholas Hilliard was written late in life. In addition to the clear italic of the name itself the rest of the writing is in the usual secretary hand employed for everyday purposes. This signature may be compared with the italic inscriptions to be found on most of the miniatures, which are probably in the painter's own hand. Since he trained as a goldsmith, these examples also link up very well with the style of inscriptions to be found on silverware of the period.

L 963–1946

7

Manuscript

A letter written in 1570 to the Earl of Lennox, Regent in Scotland, on behalf of Queen Elizabeth. The body of the letter is written in secretary, the usual everyday hand; but the Queen has signed in italic, 'Your loving frēde Elizabeth R.' The Queen, like many educated people of the time, wrote a good 'roman hand'.

$8\frac{1}{2} \times 12$ inches

FORSTER MS.190

Manuscript

A copy-sheet, probably written about 1600,
signed 'by me Thomas Carwytham'

*The first example on this copy-sheet was no doubt written
out by the writing-master: 'Cunnynge Leareninge and
sciennce which are pure by kynde. . . .' The subsequent
lines appear to have been copied, not very expertly, by his
pupil, who made no attempt to repeat the elegant
introductory initial 'C'. Like the letter written for Queen
Elizabeth, the copy is in the usual secretary hand.*

$12\frac{1}{4} \times 8\frac{1}{4}$ inches

L 1482–1945

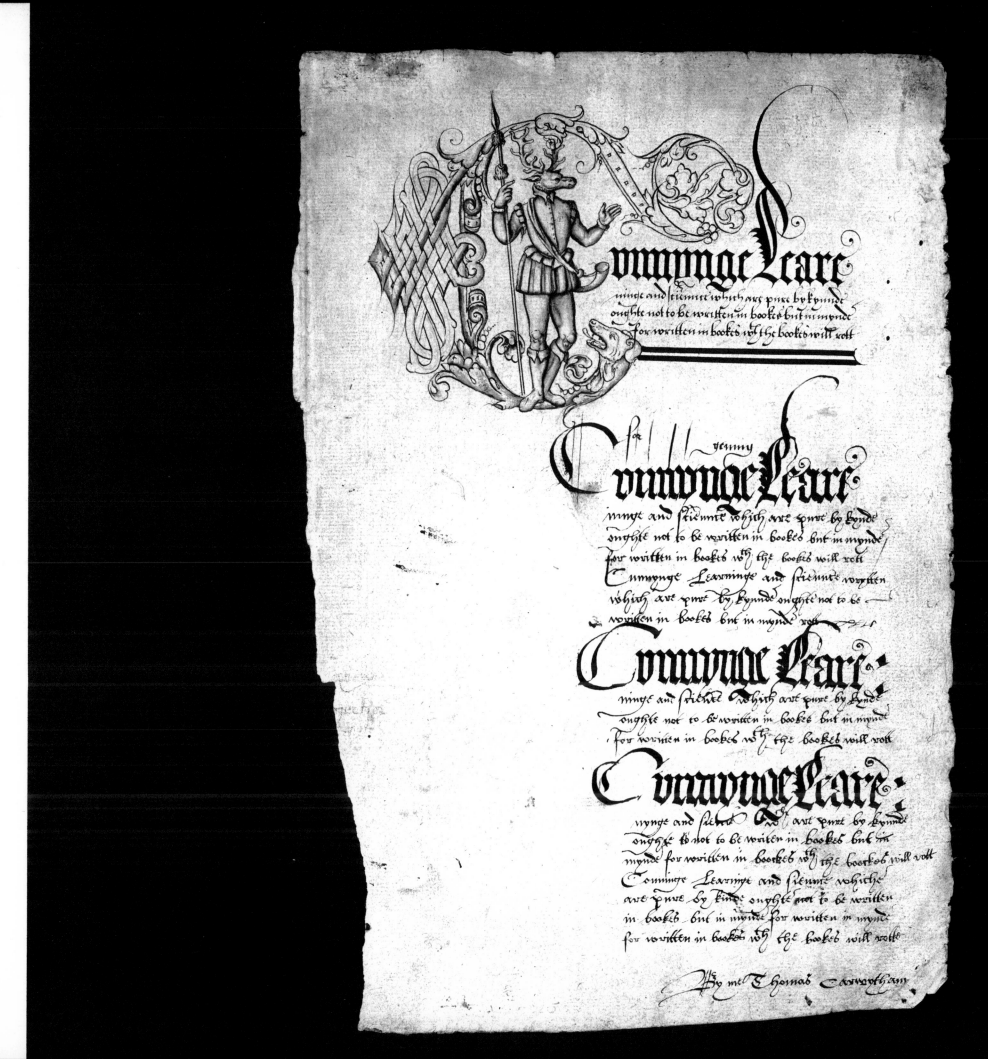

Manuscript

Letter from Lord Burghley to the Earl of Shrewsbury, with the date, 23 July 1609, written in another hand (not shown)

This letter, which was written before the publication of Billingsley's copy-book, is a typical example of an informal hand. It is not the carefully written formal epistle of the man to whom writing is part of his profession and something of a ritual; but rather a hastily dashed-off note of a friendly relationship, with all the faults and spontaneity of its modern counterpart.

$12\frac{1}{4} \times 7\frac{3}{4}$ inches

FORSTER MS.66

Manuscript

Page from a miscellaneous collection of poems,
mostly by Henry Constable (1562–1613)

*This late Elizabethan hand has a very personal style;
the development of personal hands came late in the history
of handwriting and was linked to some extent with the idea of
the importance of the individual. In this example there
appears to be a blend of both secretary and italic.*

$5\frac{1}{2} \times 3\frac{1}{2}$ inches

DYCE 44

*One of a set of twelve roundels or fruit trenchers. Painted on
wood and dated about 1590, the calligraphic inscription
has something of the same individualistic character to be
found in the poem (right), of about the same date.*

Of her excellencye both in singing
and instruments. Sonet. 4.

Not that thy hand is soft is sweete is white
Thy lipps sweete roses, breast sweet lilye is
That loue esteemes these three the chiefest blisse
Which nature euer made for lipps delight

But when these three to shew theyre heauenly might
Such wonders doe deuotion then for this
Comandeth vs, with humble zeale to kisse
Such thinges as worke miracles in oure sight

A lute of senseles wood by nature dumbe
Toucht by thy hand doth speake deuinelye well
And from thy lips and breast sweet tunes doe come
To my dead hearte the weh new life doe giue
  Of greater wonders heard we neuer tell
  Then for the dumbe to speake the dead to liue

Left page

82 CHRISTIAN.

God. to ghome be all honour ād glory.

PSAL. 94.

12 Blessed is the man whome thou chastenest (O Lorde) and teachest him in thy lawe.

13 That thou maiest giue him patience, in time of adversitie : vntill the pit be digget vp for the vngodly.

When the wicked see that all thinges goe well with them, euen in their malicious and wicked practises them they thinke them selues strayghte and happye, and to bee farre in the fauour of almightie God. But it is nothing so for

Right page

CONSOLATIONS. 83

for wee must say with the Prophet. blessed is hee which is in Gods sshoole, which loueth hys worde, and is trained vp in the same, which God maks to vs oftentimes good, sweet and comfortable by afflictions : for in them wee feele a great deale better, the force and efficacie of the diuine promises, ād being humbled, yea fighting vnder the crosse, wee learne to know oure owne weaknesse and infirmitie : In suche sorte that wee doe not exalt our selues nor trust in our owne wisedome as doeth the world, when wee are in Christes schoole, and vnder his crosse. But the man which is afflicted seeketh his

Caption

11a (above)

Manuscript

Summarie expositions upon sundrie notable sentences of the Olde Testament made in form of praiers, last quarter of the 16th century

Possibly written by Esther Inglis, daughter of a Huguenot refugee settled in Edinburgh, and one of the few well-known women calligraphers. If not actually written by her, this little book is greatly influenced by her work, and internal evidence indicates that it was certainly written in Scotland. The book contains a variety of hands showing familiarity with Continental models.

3½ × 2½ inches

L 3087–1960

11b (below)

Two of a set of six roundels or fruit trenchers, with finely written italic inscriptions round the rims. The manuscripts written by Esther Inglis are often decorated with paintings of flowers, as these flower paintings are with calligraphy.

401–1878

Manuscript

From a book containing examples of writing, mostly
in legal hands, by Richard Jackman. 1620

This delightful tour de force *occurs in a manuscript
found in one of the beams of Tangley Manor, near Guildford.
Most of the examples in the book show various legal hands,
but this cut-out in the form of an orb with a cross is
written in italic. The texts appearing in the centre of the
orb and round the edges of the cross are the Ten
Commandments.*

6 × 10½ inches

L 3051–1960

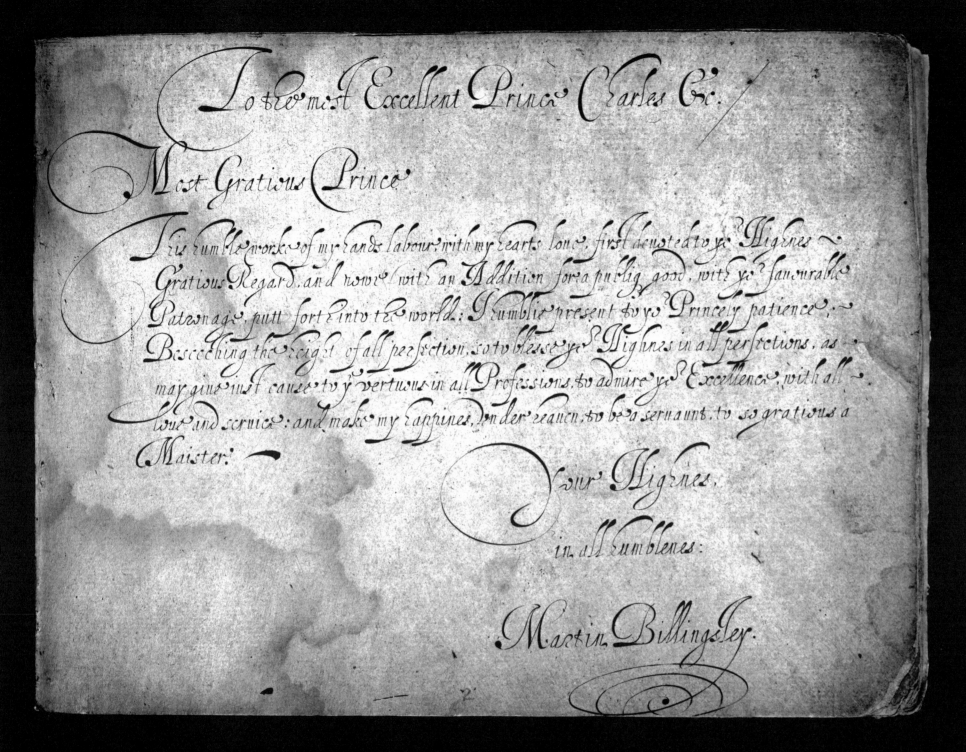

Martin Billingsley

The Pens Excellencie; or, the Secretaries Delighte. 1618

'The first English copybook of any pretensions' is Heal's description of this book. Billingsley was Writing-master to Charles I when Prince of Wales, and although his book offers a variety of hands, it was the Italian hand shown here for which he was most noted. It was also the style affected by the King.

$5\frac{1}{4} \times 7$ inches

L 3061–1960

Manuscript

A letter written by Charles I to his nephew, Prince Rupert. As Prince of Wales, the King had been a pupil of Martin Billingsley, and it is interesting to compare his mature cursive hand with the style he must have been taught in his youth.

$7\frac{1}{2} \times 5\frac{3}{4}$ inches

FORSTER MS.100

Whytchurche. 20. Oct. 1644.

Nepueu/ I am not halfe so trubled, with Sr John Winters ill lucke, as I am glad, you will be able, so soone, to March from Bristol; & that you will bring more Foode with you, then (at your being last with me) you promised: As for the reasons of my quicke Marching this way, I refer you to Digbyes relation by wch you will perceaue, there was great necessety for it, & as hitherto God hath blessed vs with successe, so I am confident you will see more & more reason for what I haue done, & that I hazarded more, if I had not hazarded as I did: So hoping to see you shortly I rest

Your loueing Oncle & most
faithfull frend
Charles R

Mount not vp to the place of Hono. lest thou be made to come downe agame w shame; for prosperitie is more damgerous then adver=~ sitie and more perish on the right hand of wordly pleasure the lefte hand of lowe degree

Billingsley

Qui se exaltat humihabitur

7

Wee are naturallie given (notwithstanding o great vn=~ worthines) to haue a marvellous good conceit of o selves y of o attons: And if so be wee can perceiue any thing in o selues to be never so little commendable or prais worthie; wee presentlie stand on tearmes, till w a Trumpett wee haue blowne forth & proclaimed y worthines of o deserte./

Pænam arrogantiæ effugit nemo .sua ➤

15a and 15b

Martin Billingsley

The Pens Excellencie; or, the Secretaries Delighte. 1618

Following Continental precedent, Billingsley offered in his book a variety of hands; even if he himself favoured the Italian, he realised that it was only one of many hands then in current use, and by no means the most popular. These illustrations show two forms of the secretary hand; the upper one influenced by the engrossing or legal hand, the lower, while showing secretary letter-forms, also seems influenced by italic.

$5\frac{1}{4} \times 7$ inches

L 3061–1960

16a and 16b

Martin Billingsley

The Pens Excellencie; or, the Secretaries Delighte. 1618

Examples of the Italian hand for which Billingsley was famous, showing both the individual letter-forms and their incorporation in a continuous piece of writing.

$5\frac{1}{4} \times 7$ inches

L 3061-1960

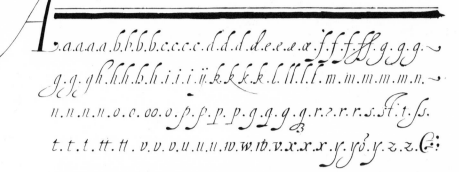

A. a. a. a. a. b. b. b. b. c. c. c. c. d. d. d. d. e. e. a. a. f. f. ff. g. g. g. g. q. qh. hh. h. h. i. i. i. i. ij. k. k. k. k. l. ll. ll. l. m. m. m. m. m. n. n. n. n. n. o. o. o. oo. o. p. p. p. p. g. g. g. q. r. r. r. r. s. ss. f. t. fs. t. t. t. tt. tt. v. v. v. u. u. u. w. w. w. x. x. x. y. yo. y. z. z. ꝯ:

A. B. C. D. E. F. G. H. I. K. L. M. N. O. P. Q. R. S. T. V. W. X. Y. Z

18

When an humour is strong and predominant, it not onlie converteth his proper nutriment, but euen that which is apt for contrarie humours, into it owne nature and qualitie. Of like force is a strong and wilfull Desire, in the minde of man: For it nott only feeds vpon agreeable motions, but makes euen those reafons, which are strongest against it, to be most for it.

Æger animus, falsa pro veris videt.

19

Richard Gething

Calligraphotechnia; or, the art of faire writing sett
forth and newly enlarged. 1642

*An unusually restrained title-page for a copy-book, in
which writing and decoration form an harmonious whole,
the actual writing being in the same style throughout.*

7 × 11 inches

L 3072–1960

Richard Gething

Calligraphotechnia; or, the art of faire writing sett forth and newly enlarged. 1642

An example of a text hand with Gothic overtones; this hand continued to be used for legal documents and even today many a will, lease or similar document has some part of its text printed in a letter-form based on this style.

7 × 11 inches

L 3072–1960

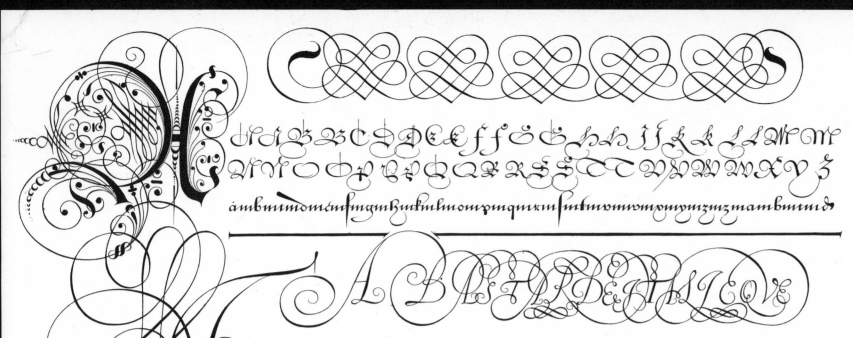

FOR that the Italian hands practized in this Kingdom haue bin, and still are corruptlie taught, especiallie by ∽ Mountebancke and circulatorie professors of impossibillities, to the dishonour of our Nation and abuse of learners in generall, being hands soe much desired, and growing more and more in vse amongst vs. For rectifieing whereof I haue in some of these my ensuing endeauours and varied examples selected, exactlie traced and followed, certaine peeces, (both in character and language) of the ablest Calligraphotechnists and ∽ Italian Mrs that euerewrot, hoping a good satisfaction to the iudicious and those, that are indulgent that waie, and for the rest, I leaue them (as they are) willfullie ignorant.

Non omnibus omnes -- GENTIAS VHICIT Gething

19

Richard Gething

Chiro-graphia; or, a booke of copies containing
sundrie examples. 1645

*Gething's pronouncement on the teaching of the Italian hand
is written in a fine example of that hand. His two important
books are grandly entitled 'Chiro-graphia' and
'Calligraphotechnia'. Gething died about 1652; the
Museum's copies of both works are those issued during the
troubled period of the Civil War.*

$7\frac{1}{2} \times 11\frac{1}{2}$ inches

1898

20

Richard Gething

Chiro-graphia; or, a booke of copies containing
sundrie examples. 1645

*A mid-17th century cursive hand, showing its employment
in a commercial and a legal document.*

$7\frac{1}{2} \times 11\frac{1}{2}$ inches

1898

John Davies

The Writing Schoolemaster. 1648

Davies died in 1618, and it is likely that his only published work appeared posthumously. It was reprinted many times, the surviving editions being mainly those issued between about 1630 and 1670. This constant reissue of copy-books, often long after the author's death, is particularly noticeable in the 17th and early 18th century, and is evidence of the persistence of older styles of handwriting into a much later period.

5¼ × 7 inches

L 3070–1960

John Davies

The Writing Schoolemaster. 1648

Two examples from John Davies's 'The Writing Schoolemaster'. It is always surprising to us that the writing-master could offer together such very different copies – one so much simpler and easier to read than the other – without concerning himself with the apparent incongruity.

5¼ × 7 inches

L 3070–1960

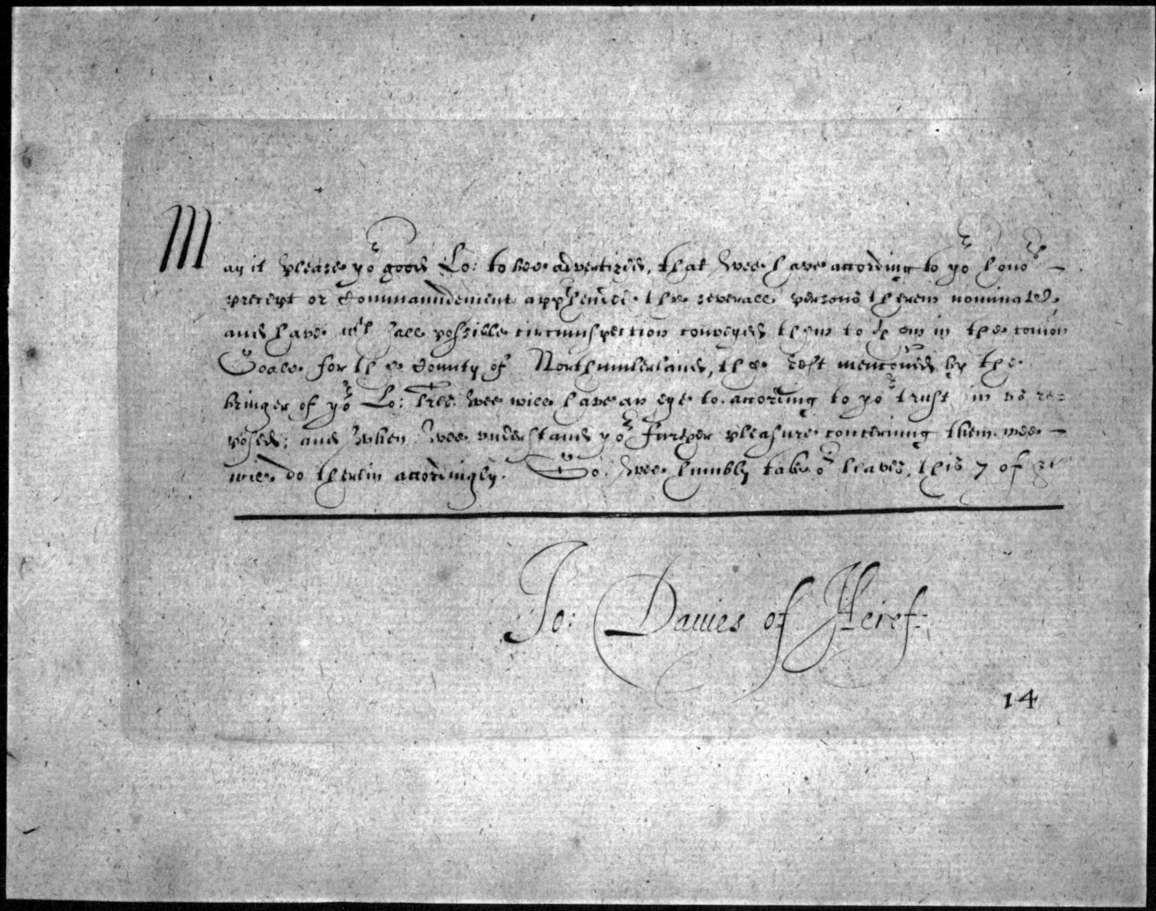

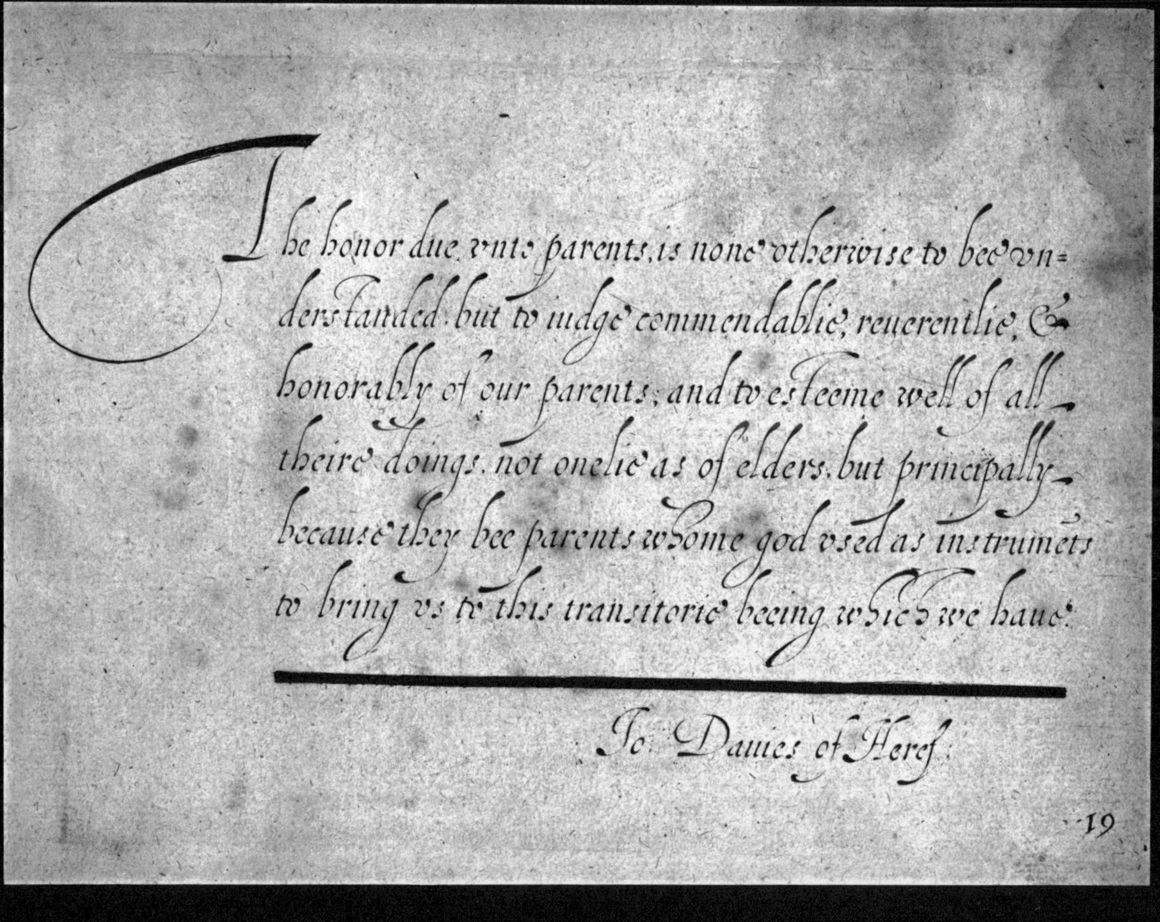

23

Edward Cocker

The Pens Transcendencie; or, faire writings labyrinth.
(1657)

*This slightly enlarged version of an engraved title-page by
Cocker is typical of his exuberance, competence – and
unblushing self-advertisement.*

$7\frac{1}{4} \times 10\frac{1}{4}$ inches

L 3064–1960

The writing-box, known as the Susan Meadows writing-desk from the name of a former owner, is dated 1665 on the lid. It is thus contemporary with much of the work of Edward Cocker, and forms an interesting parallel in its decoration with that of the engraved copy-books.

$5\frac{1}{2} \times 16\frac{1}{2} \times 11\frac{1}{4}$ inches

W 12–1955

The Portraiture of
EDWARD COCKER

Edward Cocker

One of the portraits of Edward Cocker which were often
prefaced to his works; in this one he has surrounded
himself with a characteristic piece of exuberant
penmanship. This portrait appears in 'Guide to Penmanship',
1664

$8 \times 11\frac{7}{8}$ inches

E 849–1965

Edward Cocker

Penna Volans; or, the young mans
accomplishment. 1661

*Not all Cocker's work was elaborate; when producing
copies for commercial or similar purposes he could offer a
plain unadorned style of writing. But even in this example
of a clear straightforward hand, he cannot resist a little
decorative flourish. In this he was not alone, since even
with the development of the plain commercial round hand,
the decorative bill-head continued to be favoured by the
merchant class.*

7 × 10 inches

Edward Cocker

The Pens Transcendency; or, fair writings
store-house. 1668

*The counter-attack on critics of his over-decorative style is
here carried on by Cocker in one of the little rhymes with
which he loved to adorn the harder matter of his instruction.
He makes such 'strikings' seem almost a duty: 'Some
may be drawne, as I was by delight,/In apish ffancies and so
learne to write.' He all but disarms criticism.*

7 × 10 inches

L 3058–1960

Edward Cocker

Magnum in Parvo; or, the pen's perfection. 1672

This explanatory plate by Cocker gives some idea of how the elaborate decorative initials were produced. In spite of some claims to the contrary, he does not suggest that they should be made without lifting the pen from the paper – at least not by the beginner.

6 × 8 inches

114–1889

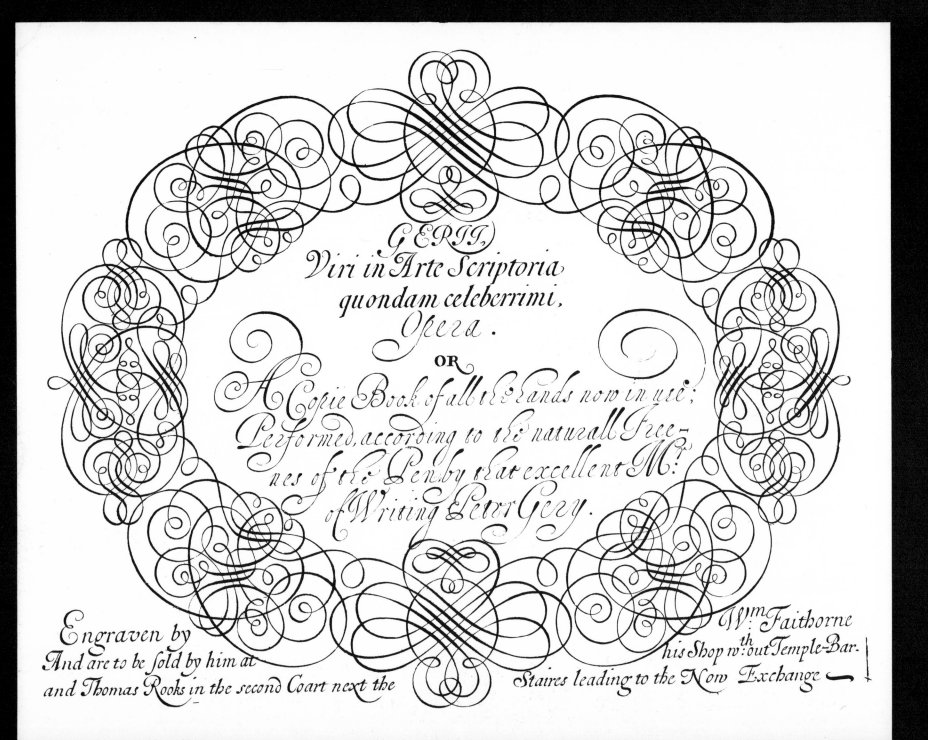

29

Peter Gery

Gerii, viri in arte scriptoria quondam celeberrimi opera; or, a copie book of all the hands now in use. 1667

Compared with his contemporary Edward Cocker, Peter Gery's work is very restrained. Nevertheless, he too cannot resist the lure of the title-page to show off, however modestly, his versatility.

$7\frac{1}{4} \times 5\frac{1}{4}$ inches

L 3082–1960

Peter Gery

Gerii, viri in arte scriptoria quondam celeberrimi opera;
or, a copie book of all the hands now in use. 1667

*An example of an unadorned page showing a commercial
text; although in the letters 'e' and 'r' the earlier
secretary hand is still traceable, the style is clear and
businesslike.*

$7\frac{1}{4} \times 5\frac{1}{4}$ inches

L 3082–1960

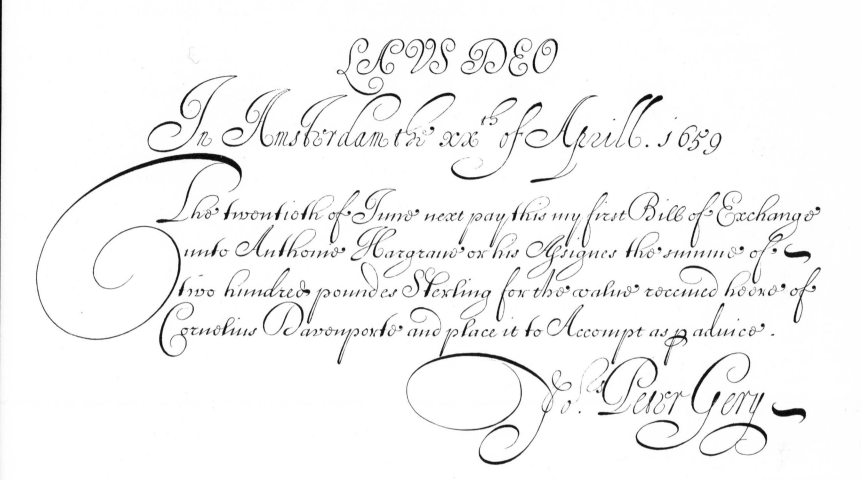

31

Peter Gery

Gerii, viri in arte scriptoria quondam celeberrimi opera;
or, a copie book of all the hands now in use. 1667

*Gery's copy-book was probably published after his death,
possibly because he was unable to satisfy himself with the
engraved results of the work.*

$7\frac{1}{4} \times 5\frac{1}{4}$ inches

L 3082–1960

Peter Gery

Gerii, viri in arte scriptoria quondam celeberrimi opera;
or, a copie book of all the hands now in use. 1667

The initial 'A', an example of the rather severe decorations
that Gery allowed himself, has more in common with the
type of initial to be found in a printed book, and sits
uncomfortably at the side of the written passage. The writing
itself is clear and bold, only allowing itself a little fancifulness
in the letter 'h'.

$7\frac{1}{4} \times 5\frac{1}{4}$ inches

L 3082–1960

ctions once resolued like fixed starres
should hold one and the same station
of firmnesse and should not be subiect
to irregular and retrograde motions

A a b b c c d d e e f g h h i k k ll mm nn
o p p g g r ss s st sp sh t tt v u w w x y z

Manuscript

Example of handwriting, with fine initials based
on older models, possibly written by John Stonestreet,
about 1688.

*The decoration of this initial 'L', finely drawn in red and
black ink, shows a jester playing on the bagpipes. A similar
initial appears in the Baildon-Beauchesne book of 1570,
and if this was indeed copied in 1688 it was already
old-fashioned. The 'L' itself was written with a broad
nib which has caused the ink to bite into the paper and spoil
the outline. The writing, though elegant and clear, is also
backward-looking; the manuscript may well illustrate
the tendency for older styles to prevail away from the
Capital and commercial interests.*

$5\frac{1}{4} \times 7\frac{3}{4}$ inches

L 3052–1960

William Elder

The Modish Penman; or, a new copy book containing variety of all the usual hands now practised in England. [*c.* 1691]

William Elder, a Scotsman working in London, was known as an engraver of portraits. In the Museum copy of 'The Modish Penman', lines of music for a wind instrument and the first lines of some songs have been written on the blank pages in a contemporary hand.

$6\frac{1}{4} \times 9\frac{1}{2}$ inches

L 3052–1960

An indicating lock of cast brass, dated about 1680. The engraved inscription includes letters which are very similar to the capitals shown in the example by William Elder.

$4\frac{2}{5} \times 6\frac{1}{5}$ inches

M 109–1926

Honours may leave their Owners Riches may
Assume Swift wings and quickly fly away
Pleasure like lightning but Salutes our Eyes
With one bright Flash and then falls Sick & dyes
But Learning and the Knowledge of rare Arts
That Man the most enjoyes that most imparts
Endeavour therefore that your Breast & Brain
The best of Learnings Treasures may retain

Humilitie is a
voluntary inclination of the Mind groun
ded upon a perfect Knowledge of our own
Condition A vertue by which a Man in
the most true consideration of his inward
Qualities maketh least Account
of himself

Thomas Watson

A Copy-book Enriched with Great Variety of the
most Useful & Modish Hands [etc.]. [*c.* 1690]

*This work by Thomas Watson, 'of Newport Pagnell' as
his title-page tells us, stands out from the other copy-books
of the period by reason of its remarkable initial letters.
The Museum copy has unfortunately been cut down and
mounted at an earlier date, but remains a large-size book.
Although reduced in these illustrations, the relative size of
the interlaced strap-work initials is obvious by comparison
with the competently written text.*

$10\frac{3}{4} \times 14\frac{1}{2}$ inches

If you aim at Advancement
be sure you have Jovem in Arca otherwise your flight to preferment without some Golden feathers will be but slow. If thou
design to be Great it matters not to be overmuch Accomplish'd, Learned,
or Wise, for wisdom many times gives a check to *Confidence*
which is the Rundle by w.ch many climb to y.e Pinacle of preferment.

It frequently happens to men truly wise
which befalls the Ears of Corn, they shoot andraise their heads high and Pert whilst
Empty, But when full and sweld with grain in Maturity begin to flag and droop,
So many having tryed all things, And not found y.t mass of Knowledge satisfaction of
so many various things, nothing but Vanity have quitted y.r Presumption owned y.r frailty.

Ayres   *Londini*

John Ayres

A Tutor to Penmanship; or, the writing master. 1698

John Ayres was one of the most successful and famous penmen of his day. 'A Tutor to Penmanship' contained a great variety of lettering and writing and was one of his best-known books. He is frequently mentioned with reverence by succeeding writing-masters, although he was also one of the participants in the unseemly battle over style which obsessed some of his notable contemporaries.

10 × 16¼ inches

1581–1880

Two-handled silver cup, parcel-gilt, dated about 1705–06.
The engraved calligraphic inscription may be compared with
the examples of writing by John Ayres of about the same
date.

$4\frac{1}{2} \times 8\frac{3}{4}$ inches

3635–1856

The Rt Honble ye Lady Leighs Bill

for a dark Culour Indian Silk Mant: & pettycoate pinking — 00 = 08 = 00 =

for making the manteau ——————————————— 00 = 08 = 00 =

Making ye New shagre Mant 8ˢ for pinking ye lining of ye same 4ˢ 00 = 12 = 00 =

Making Neece Annes Manteau 8ˢ Making Neece Marys Manteau 8ˢ . 00 = 16 = 00 =

02 = 04 = 00 =

May ye 18th 1698

Recd of ye Rt Honble ye Lady Leigh from ye hands of Mrs

Margarett Watson ye sum of two pounds & two shillens ⎫

being in full of this bill & all accounts I say so recd:— ⎬ 02 = 02 = 00 =

bay may marie mason

mem 19ˢ of ye bill belong to me

39

Manuscript

A dressmaker's bill in the name of Lady Leigh,
dated 18 May 1698

*One of a number of bills in the possession of the National
Art Library, and here used as an example of non-professional
handwriting. Three different people appear to have been
concerned in this item. The main part of the bill has been
made out according to the instructions to be found in the
copy-books, and is neatly and clearly done. The receipt of
the payment is signed (possibly by the dressmaker) in a rather
illiterate hand 'bay may (by me) Marie Mason', and
another hand has added a rough note at the bottom 'mem
19s of ye bill belong to mee'.*

4 × 7½ inches

from L427–1943

Manuscript

Letter written to James Sotheby by John Watts
from Newgate Prison, 6 October 1708

*A facetiously learned letter, written in a clear educated
hand – the writer is anxious to convey the very best impression
on all counts, since he is hoping that the recipient, James
Sotheby, will come and bail him out of prison. Quite
apart from the writer's humorous approach to his predicament,
the letter gives a very good idea of the layout and
style considered appropriate to this type of correspondence.*

8 × 6 inches

L 1768–1966

Sr   Octob: 6th: 1708:

'ΗΈΛΙΟΣ: hath 4 Times, and ΜΉΝΗ 52 Times Transited MAZZAROTH
Since my Immurem.t in Castles Inchanted: About three years Past
you was pleased to make a Descent, visiting me in Limbo &c: for w.ch
kindness I sent a Letter of thanks, till Acknowledgm.t could be made
in Propriâ Personâ, but was Obstructed: for this Arke of my Body
hath ever since been so Agitated, by the Adverse Billows of Fortune
and Gradated from Schools to Colledges, and now at the Vniversity of
Januæ Novæ am Commencing Doctour, in the great Quadrangle
there called Debtors Hall. And if you are yet in the Land of the
Living, as for certain I that write am in the dons, and you can
Descend also in Tartaro, where no one but a Hercules in Good
will dare Attempt; Cerberus will Admitt you, without y.e Fatigue
of Carrying him away at y.e Return: Excuse this Freedom knowing
the man, at Present in Nubibus, Sed post Nubila PHŒBUS: I hope
the Time may be short, and to Contemplate on the ARCANA's of this
Infernall Region are not so Terrifying, as y.r Presence will be
Exhilerating to him S.r who was, is, and shall Remain:

This Gent: a Quondam Sufferer w.th my self,
can Satisfie how I came here, & the Reason
of Imploring Auxilium Deorum ———
Ο' ΜΗΎΡΟΥ ΙΛΙΑΆΟΣ ———

y.r Humb: Serv.t to Command:

John: Watts·

Value not thy self overmuch lest
thou loose the good opinion of
others. For self estimation is more
like to cause contempt & envy
than to get admiration & honor.

Seddon

41 (left)

John Seddon

The Pen-man's Paradis, both pleasant & profitable.
1695

Seddon was greatly appreciated by his contemporaries. His decoration, done with 'one continued and entire tract of the pen' is reminiscent of Edward Cocker, but there is never quite so much unrelated tangle as in the earlier master. William Massey wrote of him in 1763, 'he exceeds all our English penmen in a fruitful fancy, and surprizing invention in the ornamental parts of his writing'.

$14 \times 8\frac{3}{4}$ inches

II. iv. 1872

42 (right)

A portrait of George Shelley engraved by George Bickham. In addition to the books which he had already published, the picture also displays the implements of the writing-master's trade – his pens, pen-knife and ink-well.

$11\frac{5}{8} \times 7\frac{5}{8}$ inches

E 866–1965

To the Honble. the Governor Deputy-Governor and Directors of the Bank of England

Sr. Gilbert Heathcote Kt. and Ald. Governor,
Nathaniel Gould Esq Deputy-Governor,

SIR James Bateman, *Kt. & Ald.*	John Rudge, *Esq;*
Mr. Gerard Conyers.	*Sir* William Scawen, *Kt.*
Josiah Diston, *Esq;*	John Smith, *Esq; of B. Buildings.*
Mr. John De Vinck.	John Ward, *Esq; Ald.*
Mr. James Dolliffe.	William Des Bouverie *Esq;*
Mr. John Emilie.	*Mr.* Peter Delme.
Mr. John Gould.	*Mr.* William Dawsonne.
Sir William Hodges, *Bar.*	Francis Eyles, *Esq;*
Sir John Houblon, *Kt. & Ald.*	William Gore, *Esq;*
Sir Theodore Janssen, *Kt.*	*Mr.* John Hanger.
Samuel Lethieullier, *Esq;*	Thomas Scawen, *Esq;*
Sir Charles Peers, *Kt. & Ald.*	*Mr.* John Shipman.

Your Honours having from an Exact Judgment made choice of the most Accomplish'd Penmen and Accountants in Europe, induc'd me to believe y̆ this peice of Penmanship might be favour'd with yo.r Acceptance; Espescialy Since the Greatest Masters of my Profession have readily alow'd it to be y̆ best yet Publish'd. And as J hope you'l pardon the Liberty J have taken in prefixing your Names to it; So you'l permit me to tell the World how much J wish the Bank of England may be always under the Conduct of such Governors & Directors, whose uncomon Zeal to her Majesties Government, and the Protestant Jnterest, has not only surpriz'd, but discourag'd the Enemies of Both.

Yor. Hono.rs most Obed.t & very hum.bll. Serv.t

George Shelley.

43 (left)

George Shelley

Natural Writing in all the Hands, with Variety of Ornament. (1709)

George Shelley and Charles Snell were almost contemporaries, and both were educated at Christ's Hospital, whose writing school was well known. In spite of, or because of this, they became rivals in their profession, and as mentioned elsewhere, their differences were both bitter and vocal.

$9\frac{1}{4} \times 14\frac{1}{4}$ inches

2035–1884

44 (right)

George Shelley

Natural Writing in all the Hands, with Variety of Ornament. (1709)

An example of the bold simple hand which was considered particularly suited for commercial use, and which in its later developments was to supplant all other hands for this purpose.

$9\frac{1}{4} \times 14\frac{1}{4}$ inches

2035–1884

There is nothing more certain than
Death; nothing more uncertain than
the time of dying: I will therefore always
be prepar'd for y[t] which may come at.....
anytime.

Shelley

George Shelley

Natural Writing in all the Hands, with Variety of Ornament. (1709)

Even his opponents admitted Shelley's superiority in all versions of the round hand; it was his continued interest in the 'sprigg'd fancies' which aroused such passion. In the cleverly contrived birds of this example his work is reminiscent of earlier masters.

$9\frac{1}{4} \times 14\frac{1}{4}$ inches

2035–1884

George Shelley

Natural Writing in all the Hands, with Variety of Ornament. (1709)

However plain the main body of the text might be, the elaborate initial letter continued to be favoured, even by those who regretted such frivolities in writing as a whole. The influence of this aspect continued to be found quite late in the 19th century in the persistence of elaborately engraved bill-heads.

$9\frac{1}{4} \times 14\frac{1}{4}$ inches

2035–1884

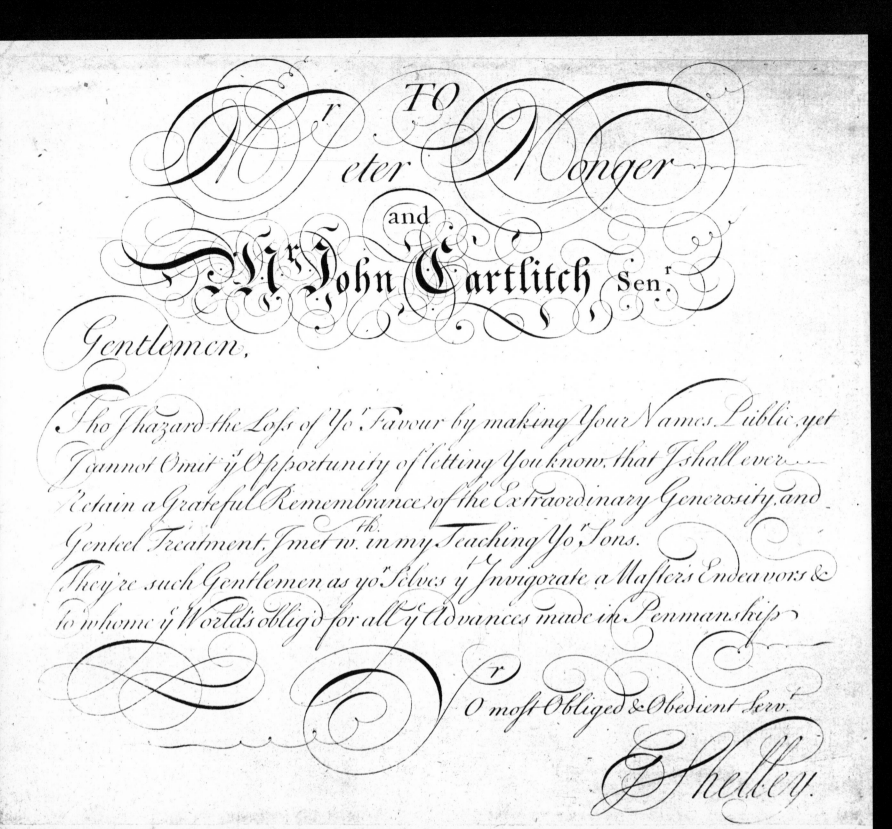

George Shelley

Penna Volans, after yᵉ English, French & Dutch way. [c. 1710]

A form of self-advertisement, which, in one way or another, all writing-masters loved to include in their works. Although in this example the elaborate letter-head is meant as an example to be copied by hand, it is typical of the engraved bill- or letter-head of the 18th century whose inspiration lies directly with the copy-books.

7¾ × 11 inches

L 537-1939

Charles Snell

The Art of Writing in its Theory and Practice. 1712

Charles Snell, the great opponent of George Shelley, tried to formulate 'standard rules' for writing, based on a mathematical approach to letter-forms. His attempt was not the first, nor was it to be the last.

9 × 14 inches

L 599–1879

Sr   Jan.ry 5.th 1711.

If you would attain to an Excellency in Writing. Affect not new invented Forms of Letters, and throw not Strokes through the Bodies of those you use: This will preserve Its Legibility: Let your Letters be adapted to the most easy way of Joyning: This will make your Hand Expeditious. And if a Delicacy & Spirit appear in your Strokes, and a due regard be had to the Proportion of Letters, Words, and Lines; your Writing will appear Beautiful ———

Yoᵘʳˢ C Snell.

1 2 3 4 5 6 7 8 9

ee, ei, oo, ic, on, ni, in, is, ix.

Charles Snell

The Art of Writing in its Theory and Practice. 1712

In spite of Snell's concern for the purity of writing, even he cannot resist a certain amount of flourish and decoration in his hands. Perhaps the suggestion, made in the course of the famous controversy, that those who objected to flourishes did so because they themselves were not competent to make them, made it imperative to show that, if required, the writing-master was proficient in all aspects of his art.

9 × 14 inches

L 599–1879

Nmnn,
Omooo,
Pmpp,
Qmqu,
Rmrr,
Smfss,

Before thou enterest upon any Action, consider not only whether it be Lawful, but whether it be Expedient: that may be Lawful in it self, but not at such a time; or perchance not at all to thee; a Circumstance alters the Case & makes an action sinful. What is one Mans Meat, is another Mans poyson: In doing a Good Action &c.

Vive La Plume :1711:

Sir By Order & for accompt of Monsieur Gineau of Hambourg I have this day drawn on you 1000 Crowns to yᵉ Order of Benajah Lommineaux, & 800 Crowns to yᵉ Order of Pierre Mauvillain, at 75 ßat 2us I Recommend to you the honour of my Bils, & if you have not yet yᵉ Necessary Orders from the sd Mons. &c.

Tmttu,
Vllou,
Wmw,
Xmx,
Ymyy,
Zmz,

50

Charles Snell

The Art of Writing in its Theory and Practice. 1712

An example of a suitable business hand, showing also the appropriate layout of the text to be copied. Although the first example of this type of copy to be shown here, many variations on this theme are to be found in all the copy-books of the period, and they play an increasingly dominant part as the century progresses.

9 × 14 inches

L 599–1879

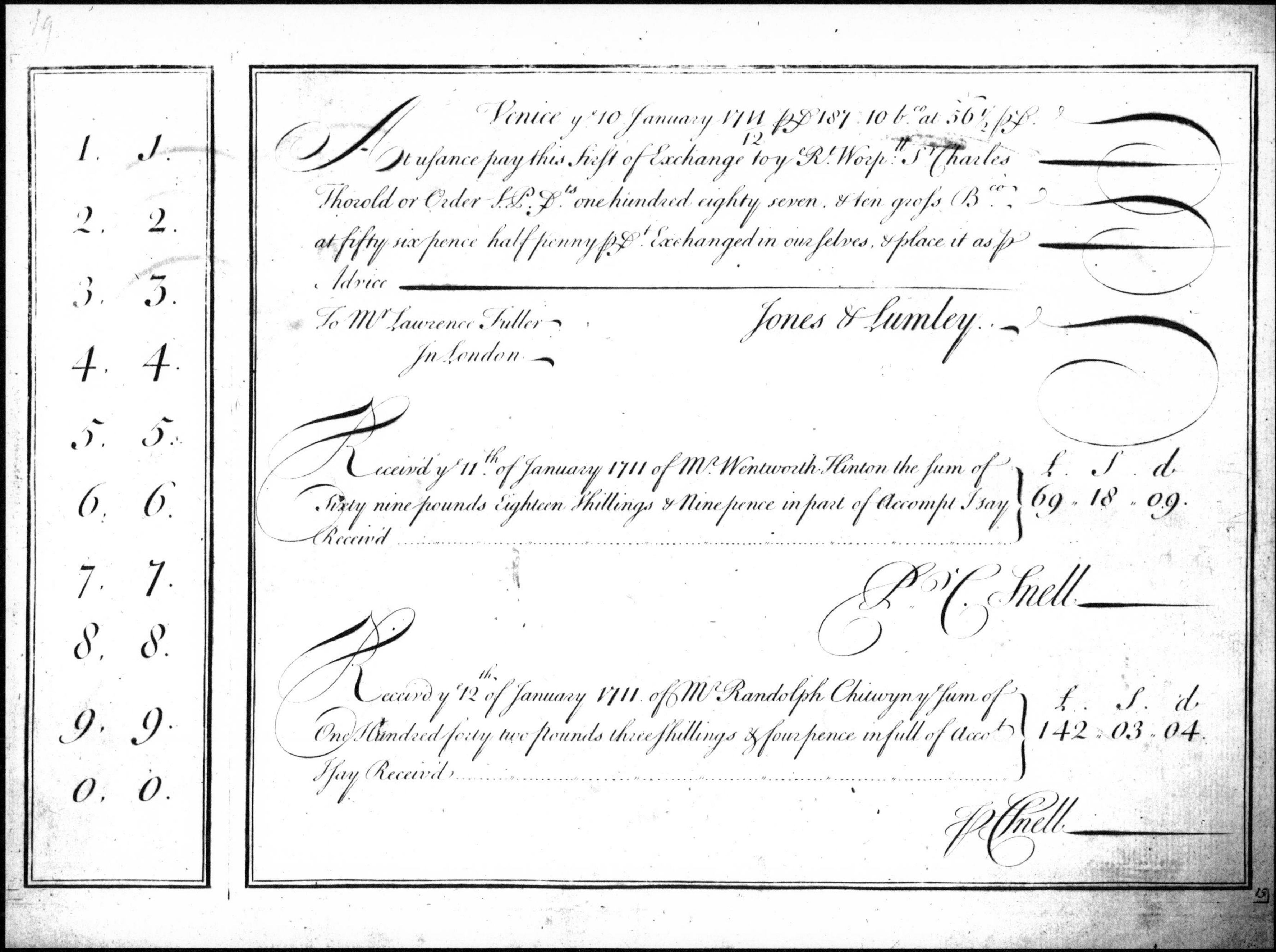

1. 1.
2. 2.
3. 3.
4. 4.
5. 5.
6. 6.
7. 7.
8. 8.
9. 9.
0. 0.

Venice yᵉ 10 January 1711/12 pᵈ 187 : 10 bᶜᵒ at 56½ pᵈ

At usance pay this First of Exchange to yᵉ Rᵗ Worpˡˡ Sʳ Charles Thorold or Order Lᵈ. Pᵈˢ one hundred eighty seven, & ten gross Bᶜᵒ at fifty six pence half penny pᵈ. Exchanged in our selves, & place it as p Advice

To Mʳ Lawrence Fuller
In London

Jones & Lumley.

Receiv'd yᵉ 11ᵗʰ of January 1711 of Mʳ Wentworth Hinton the sum of Sixty nine pounds Eighteen Shillings & Nine pence in part of Accompt I say Receiv'd

£	s	d
69	18	09

Pʳ C. Snell

Receiv'd yᵉ 12ᵗʰ of January 1711 of Mʳ Randolph Chitwyn yᵉ sum of One Hundred forty two pounds three Shillings & four pence in full of Accᵗ I say Receiv'd

£	s	d
142	03	04

C. Snell

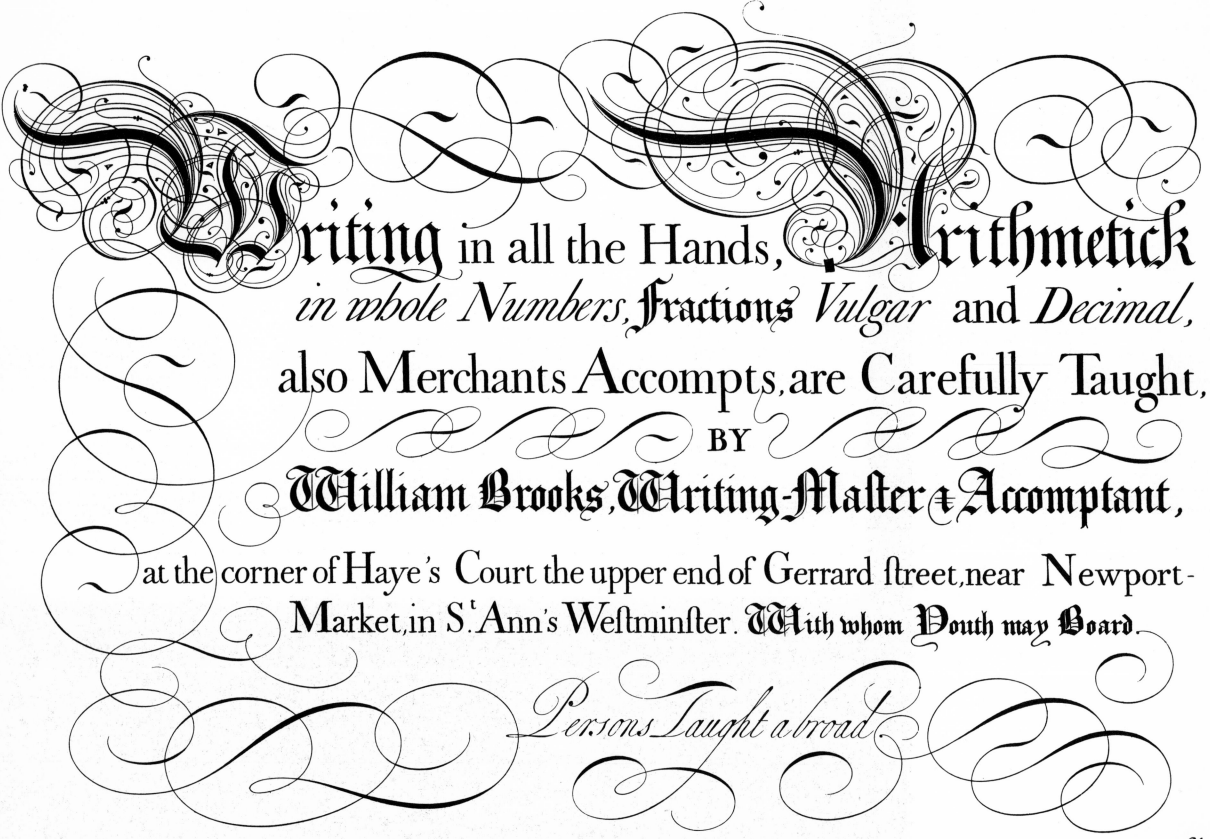

Writing in all the Hands, Arithmetick in whole Numbers, Fractions Vulgar and Decimal, also Merchants Accompts, are Carefully Taught, BY William Brooks, Writing-Master & Accomptant, at the corner of Haye's Court the upper end of Gerrard street, near Newport-Market, in St Ann's Westminster. With whom Youth may Board.

Persons Taught abroad.

William Brooks

A Delightful Recreation for the Industrious. 1717

A form of self-promotion: Brooks displays his virtuosity by the variety of hands shown in his advertisement. It also gives an indication of the number of styles still current at this period, before the overriding demands of commerce swamped the less practical ones.

$9\frac{3}{4} \times 14\frac{1}{2}$ inches

L 1744–1922

William Brooks

A Delightful Recreation for the Industrious. 1717

This charming address to the ladies, written in the Italian hand considered (as Brooks points out) so particularly suited to the fair sex, reminds one of the rather blunter remarks on the subject recorded by Billingsley one hundred years earlier (see p. xiv)

$9\frac{3}{4} \times 14\frac{1}{2}$ inches

L 1744–1922

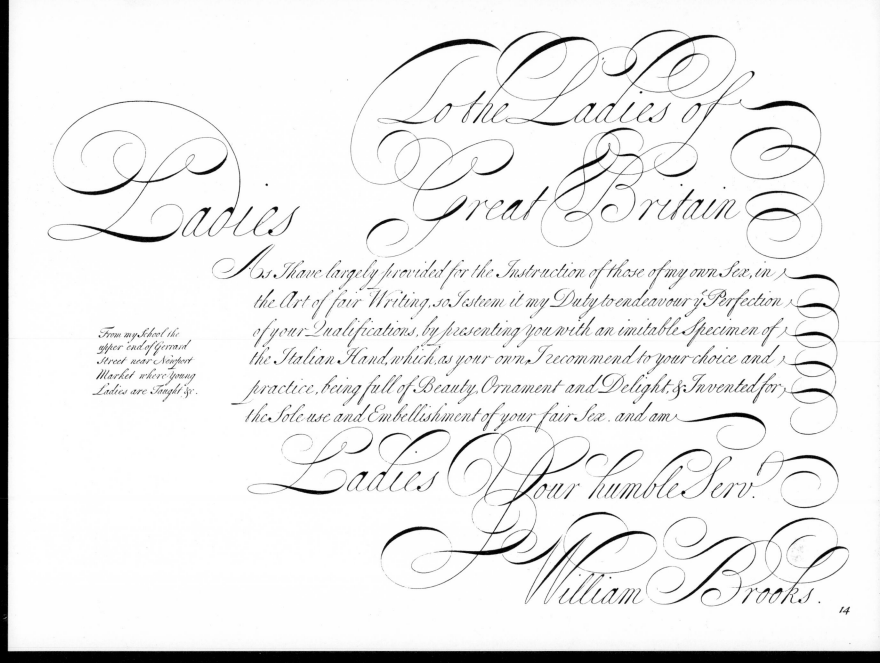

14

Remember thy Creator in the days of thy Youth

Shew faithfulness to thy friend, and equity to all

The fear of the Lord is the begining of wisdom

Virtue alone is immortal when all things perish

Works of Piety must never go without Humility

Xenophon's Prudence and Conduct were admirable

Youth well instructed makes Age well disposed

Zeal in a good Cause is very commendable

9

William Brooks

A Delightful Recreation for the Industrious. 1717

Of this type of copy, to become almost the standard form of teaching, William Brooks writes: 'The pieces in this book are adapted to the proper length of . . . books wherein children usually write at school, and to render them more practicable are so contrived that they may be cut asunder and laid before the learner, one piece only at a time, till he is master of one hand before he enter upon another.'

$9\frac{3}{4} \times 14\frac{1}{2}$ inches

L 1744–1922

The lid of a silver box of about 1685; the illustration
has been greatly enlarged in order to show clearly the
calligraphic inscription added at a later date on the underneath
side of the box (below).

3 × 3 inches

M 700–1926

Let Decency be observ'd in all your Actions and Discourse; Never study to be Diverting without being useful; let no Jest intrude upon good Manners; nor say any thing that may offend a Chast Ear. Never talk over much of what you know; least you be suspected to talk of what you do not know: And, Remember, that tho' Silence is not always the Mark of a Wise man, yet Noise and Impertinence do certainly discover the Fool. Aam, bm, cm, dm, em, fm, gm, hm, im, jm, km, lm,

Entertain Honour with Humility; Poverty with Patience; Blessings with Thankfulness; & Afflictions with Resignation. Give your Heart to your Creator; Reverence to your Superiors; Honour to your Parents; Your Bosom to your Friend; Diligence to your Calling; Ear to good Counsel; and Alms to the Poor. T. Weston scr.

55

Thomas Weston

A Copy-book Written for the Use of the Young-Gentlemen at the Academy in Greenwich. 1726

This work by Thomas Weston, sub-titled 'Book of writing, drawing and ancient arithmetic', is usually found bound with two other works by him. Most writing-masters found it expedient to combine the teaching of handwriting with one or more other subjects, and arithmetic (or less frequently drawing) was a particularly favoured combination, for obvious reasons. The first of the 'three R's' was not usually associated with writing.

$18 \times 11\frac{1}{2}$ inches

19. ix. 1863

Thomas Weston

A Copy-book Written for the Use of the
Young-Gentlemen at the Academy in Greenwich.
1726

*An interesting example showing the technique of
forming letters which Weston recommended to 'the
young-gentlemen at the Academy in Greenwich'. The idea
of fitting letters into the form of an 'o' has a long history; the
angle of slope and the relative position of the 'thicks' and
'thins' has, however, varied.*

18 × 11½ inches

19. ix. 1863

Commerce.

Trade and a well regulated Commerce flourishes by
Multitudes, and gives Employment to all its Professors:
Fleets of Merchant-men are so many Squadrons of
Floating Shops, that vend our Wares & Manufactures
in all the Markets of the World, and, with Dangerous
Industry, find out Chapmen under both the Tropicks.

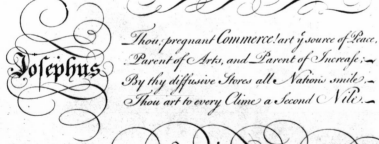

Thou, pregnant Commerce! art y source of Peace,
Parent of Arts, and Parent of Increase:
By thy diffusive Stores all Nations smile,
Thou art to every Clime a Second Nile.

Scripsit.

57

George Bickham

The Universal Penman. (1743)

George Bickham's 'Universal Penman', originally issued in parts, is one of the most splendid writing-books ever published. Bickham conceived the idea of collecting examples of writing from all the best masters of his day, and adorning the plates with a variety of ornament and genre scenes. He was himself a competent engraver and was much in demand for writing-books as well as other types of work. The volume is planned on a large scale, consisting of 212 engraved folio plates, and was reissued a number of times as well as being published in an abridged form. It contains every type of current hand, as well as advice on the technique and principles of handwriting, together with useful advice and moral precepts for the would-be successful man of business and his clerk.

$16\frac{1}{4} \times 10\frac{1}{2}$ inches

L 3084–1960

George Bickham

The Universal Penman. (1743)

This plate from 'The Universal Penman' was probably written out as well as engraved by George Bickham, himself no mean penman. The illustration at the top of the page gives a charming picture of a writing-master and pupils at work, and is typical of the little scenes scattered throughout the book.

$16\frac{1}{4} \times 10\frac{1}{2}$ inches

L 3084–1960

ON Promiffory Notes.

A Promiffory Note mentioning Order *is indorfible from one Perfon to another; which is done by the prefent Poffeffor's writing his Name on the Back of it, and delivering it up to the Party, to whom he intends to affign over his Property therein.*

It is unneceffary to have a Promiffory Note payable to Bearer *indorfed, if you are fatisfy'd the Note is good: And if a Note be indorfed, it is neceffary to write a Receipt thereon, to prevent its being negociated, after it is paid and deliver'd up.*

If the Drawer of a Note refufes Payment, the Note is good againft the Indorfer. The delivering up a Promiffory Note to the Perfon who fign'd it is a fufficient Voucher of its being paid, nor is there any Occafion of writing a Receipt thereon.

Promiffory Notes, and Book-Debts, if not legally demanded in fix Years, cannot be recover'd by Law: And if you keep a Promiffory Note upon Demand, in your own Hands above three Days, and the Perfon it's upon fhould fail, the Lofs will be your own; but if he fail within the three Days it will light on the Perfon that paid it you. Let all Notes be made for Value receiv'd, and in the Form of thefe that follow.

G. Bickham Fecit.

N.° XXXV.   MDCCXXXVIII.

THE

Penmans Advice

To Young Gentlemen.

Ye British Youths, our Age's Hope & Care;
You whom the next may polish, or impair;
Learn by the Pen those Talents to insure,
That fix ev'n Fortune, & from Want secure;
You with a dash in time may drain a Mine;
And deal the Fate of Empires in a Line;
For Ease and Wealth, for Honour & Delight,
Your Hands yo.r Warrant, if you well can Write.
"True ease in Writing comes from Art, not Chance;
"As those move easiest, who have learn'd to Dance.

To Young Ladies

Ye springing Fair, whom gentle Minds incline,
To all that's curious, innocent, and fine!
With Admiration in your Works are read
The various Textures of the twining Thread.
Then let the Fingers, whose unrivall'd Skill,
Exalts the Needle, grace the Noble Quill.
An artless Scrawl y.e blushing Scribler shames;
All shou'd be Fair that Beauteous Woman frames.
Strive to excell, with Ease the Pen will move;
And pretty Lines add Charms to infant Love.

Samuel Vaux scrip.

17 34.

G. Bickham sculp.

George Bickham

The Universal Penman. (1743)

This plate from 'The Universal Penman', by one of the lesser known writing-masters of the day, shows the general level of competence, as well as a charming calligraphic head- and tail-piece. The passage 'To Young Ladies' seems to have been very popular; it appears in other similar works and a manuscript version, written out by Miss Mary Roberts, a pupil at 'Mr. Massey's Academy', 1792, is in the present author's possession.

$16\frac{1}{4} \times 10\frac{1}{2}$ inches

L 3084–1960

George Bickham

The Universal Penman. (1743)

Another plate from 'The Universal Penman', showing the persistence of decorative lettering which is characteristic of so many plates in this work; even though the book is aimed primarily at the man of business and his clerk, the writing-master cannot resist the opportunity to display his virtuosity.

$16\frac{1}{4} \times 10\frac{1}{2}$ inches

L 3084–1960

THE

Writing Masters

INVITATION, *AND* INSTRUCTION.

Come Youths this Charming Sight behold!
With Laurel Plum'd, a Pen of Gold!
If You would win this Glorious Prize,
Do as Your Master shall Advise;
Till You, from Learners, Masters grown,
Make both the Bays & Gold your Own.

Come Listen Youths, and I'll Display
To this Rare Art a Certain Way.
He that in Writing would Improve,
Must first with Writing fall in Love;
For True Love for True Pains will call,
And that's the Charm that Conquers All.

Three things bear mighty Sway with Men, | Who can the least of these Command,
The Sword, the Scepter, and the P E N; | In the First Rank of Fame will Stand.

Labor Omnia Vincit.

J. Champion   delin. et sculp.

Nº IX.   G.B. sculp.

John Langton

A New Copy-book of the Italian-Hand. (1727)

Although this is the title-page of a work called 'A new copy-book of the small Italian-hand', John Langton has nevertheless taken the opportunity to display his versatility in a great variety of the hands then in use. His title-page thus becomes an advertisement for the writing-master as well as for the book. But although he takes into account the varied needs of his prospective pupils, he does not find it necessary to attract them with over-decorative styles and flourishes.

$7\frac{1}{2} \times 12\frac{1}{4}$ inches

L 1397–1922

William Chinnery

Writing and Drawing made Easy, Amusing and
Instructive. (The Compendious Emblematist.) 1750

*This work, 'more like a thing designed for amusement, than
any improvement in the hands', consists of moral texts
illustrating the 'emblem' engraved on the opposite page.
Judging by the number of surviving editions, this charming
work must have been very popular, though possibly its
appeal was limited to 'the female practitioners of the art'.
In this work, as in Bickham's 'Universal Penman', reference
is made to the allied art of drawing; other writing-masters
with a more practical appeal in mind, linked writing with
arithmetic, and frequently offered to teach both subjects –*

*indeed Cocker's 'Arithmetic', starting out in the 17th
century had a long and honourable life until well into the
19th century.*

$6\frac{1}{2} \times 7$ inches

L 3066–1960

Mrs Jemima Williamson

Bought of Samuel Tompion

1750.		s	£ . s . d
May 5	10½ Yards Yorkshire Cloth	at 6 . 4 ₱ Yard	3 . 6 . 6 .
	7 Yards Spanish Black	at 16 . 3	5 . 13 . 9 .
	6¾ Yards fine grey Cloth	at 15 . 7	5 . 5 . 2 .
	16½ Yards second Drab	at 15 . 6	12 . 15 . 9 .
	5⅞ Yards Superfine Spanish Cloth	at 18 . 5	5 . 8 . 1 .
	4 Yards Frieze	at 3 . 6	— . 14 . — .
	31 Yards Livery Scarlet Cloth	at 13 . —	20 . 3 . — .
		£	53 . 6 . 3 .

Lloyd script.

63 (left)

Edward Lloyd

The Young Merchant's Assistant. (1751)

After the knots and 'strikings' of the earlier period, and the pious sentences and classical allusions, business methods and the plain round hand begin to take precedence. The titles of the books, too, become plain and straightforward, indicative of the matter within. Lloyd himself advertises this work as 'Containing a great variety of curious specimens of the most useful parts of penmanship for the more ready despatch of public business.'

$9\frac{1}{2} \times 14\frac{1}{2}$ inches

L 534–1939

64 (right)

A bill dated 3 July 1786. It shows the calligraphic form of the engraved head-piece, and then, below, the actual account in manuscript. The handwritten part bears a good resemblance to the correct forms as shown in the copy-books, but the signature of the receipt, written in another hand, is less sure of itself.

4×8 inches

L 427–1943

A
New Copy Book
OF
Round Text.
Half Text and small Hand.
By
Samuel Ȝ Arthur Writing Master
in
EDINBURGH

A. Bannerman Sculp.ᵗ

65 (left)

Samuel McArthur

A New Copy-Book of Round Text, Half Text and Small Hand. [c. 1755]

Of Samuel McArthur, 'writing master in Edinburgh', very little is known; even the exact date of his published copy-book is uncertain. This charming title-page with its Rococo frame and fancy lettering is in great contrast to the businesslike approach of so many of his contemporaries.

$9\frac{1}{4} \times 14\frac{3}{4}$ inches

L 533–1939

66 (right)

Samuel McArthur

A New Copy-Book of Round Text, Half Text and Small Hand. [c. 1755]

This is the type of copy which was to become increasingly popular. A variety of hands is still offered, but it has become a limited variety, and all with the same end in view, namely a clear, quick hand suitable for business purposes; at the same time inculcating good commercial practice rather than moral virtues – unless they appeared to be one and the same thing.

$9\frac{1}{4} \times 14\frac{3}{4}$ inches

L 533–1939

Mend thy manners

Money commands many enjoyments

Many are the annoyances that accompany Mans Life

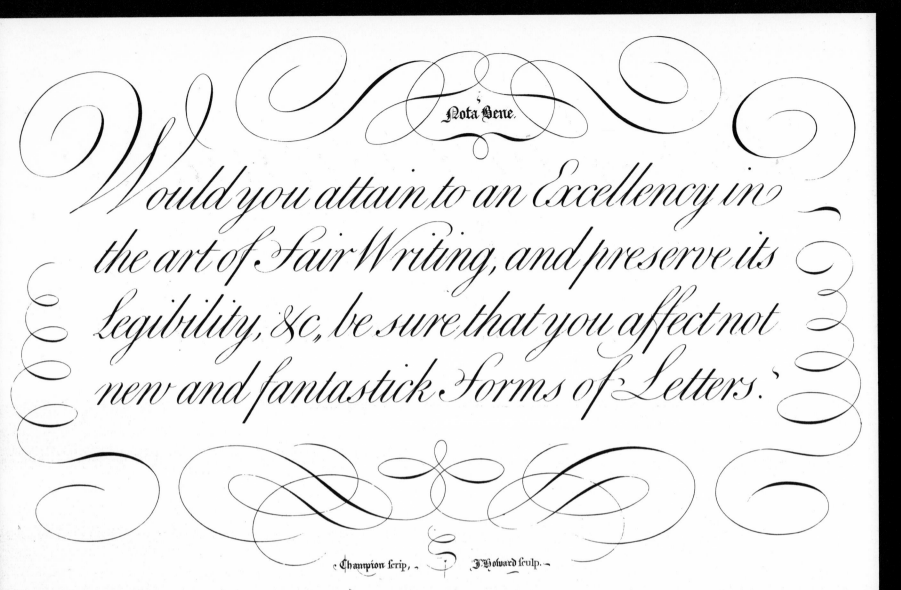

Nota Bene.

Would you attain to an Excellency in the art of Fair Writing, and preserve its legibility, &c., be sure that you affect not new and fantastick Forms of Letters.

Champion scrip,   J. Holward sculp.

Joseph Champion

The Penman's Employment. 1763

Joseph Champion was highly regarded by his contemporaries, and he contributed a number of plates to Bickham's 'The Universal Penman'. This example gives advice on handwriting in a suitably sober style.

$9\frac{3}{4} \times 15$ inches

16. iv. 1875

68

Joseph Champion

The Penman's Employment. 1763

An interesting example of suiting style to content – a simple straightforward handwriting suggesting the same qualities in the writer, with just a slight flourish to indicate competence in such matters should it be required.
9¾ × 15 inches

16. iv. 1875

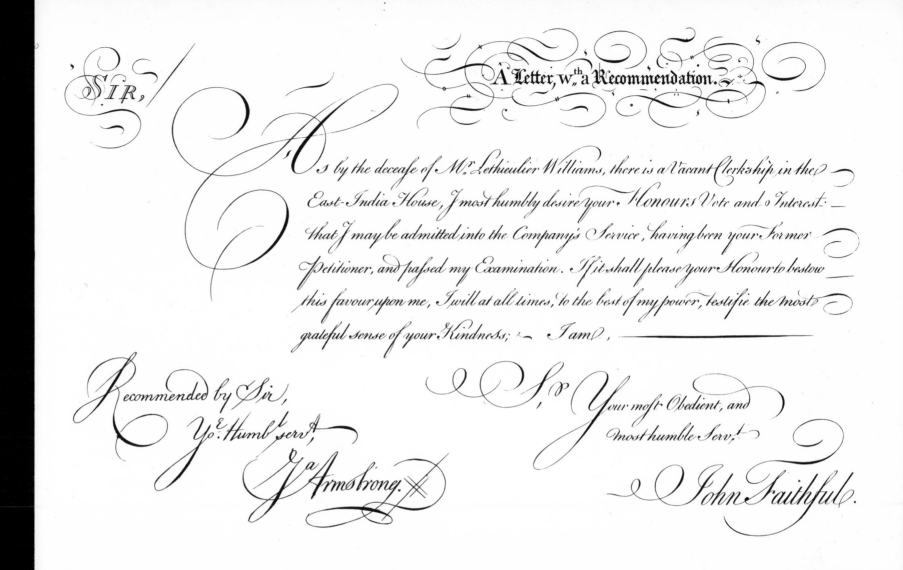

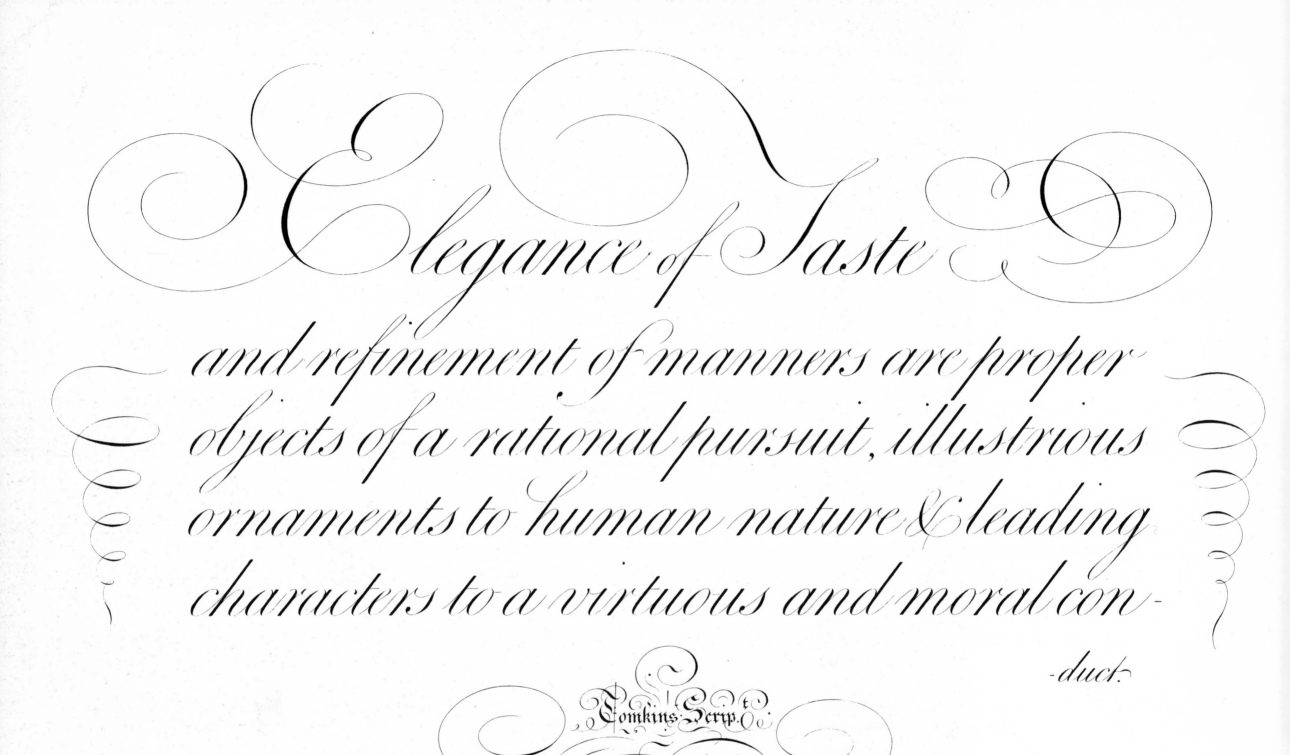

Elegance of Taste

and refinement of manners are proper
objects of a rational pursuit, illustrious
ornaments to human nature & leading
characters to a virtuous and moral con-

-duct.

Tomkins Script.

J.Ellis sc.

Publifhed as the Act directs. 19.May 1777.

69 (left)

Thomas Tomkins

The Beauties of Writing. 1777

Thomas Tomkins was a friend of Sir Joshua Reynolds (who painted his portrait) and many other celebrities of the day. A new edition of 'The Beauties of Writing' appeared as late as 1844, so little did the basic style of English handwriting change during that period.

$11 \times 17\frac{1}{2}$ inches

L 1787–1951

70 (right)

The portrait of Thomas Tomkins: a mezzotint by Charles Turner from the portrait by Sir Joshua Reynolds. The writing-master's equipment should also be noted.

14×10 inches

E 874–1965

Avoid bad companions. d.

Beware of ostentation. w

Confine your passions. ma

Deride no infirmities. ak.

Endeavour to improve. m,

Fear attends the guilty. m,

Duncan Smith

The Academical Instructor. 1794

In this example by Duncan Smith it is already possible to see the weakness in this style of writing, which, carried to excess by some practitioners, was to lead to illegibility. It was caused by undue emphasis on the thick and thin strokes, which made a part of each letter disappear altogether. The Library also possesses a copy-book apparently based on another work by Duncan Smith but published in Russia. This is further indication of the importance of the English business hand, and the need for countries trading with England to be familiar with it.

$9 \times 11\frac{1}{2}$ inches

Joseph Webb

Webb's Useful Penmanship. 1796

Even in the few years which separate this work from Edward Lloyd's 'The Young Merchant's Assistant' of 1751 (plate 63), a further simplification of forms is perceptible. Any unnecessary flourishing is cut down to a minimum – the content and its clear presentation is paramount.

$7\frac{1}{4} \times 11\frac{1}{4}$ inches

L 542–1939

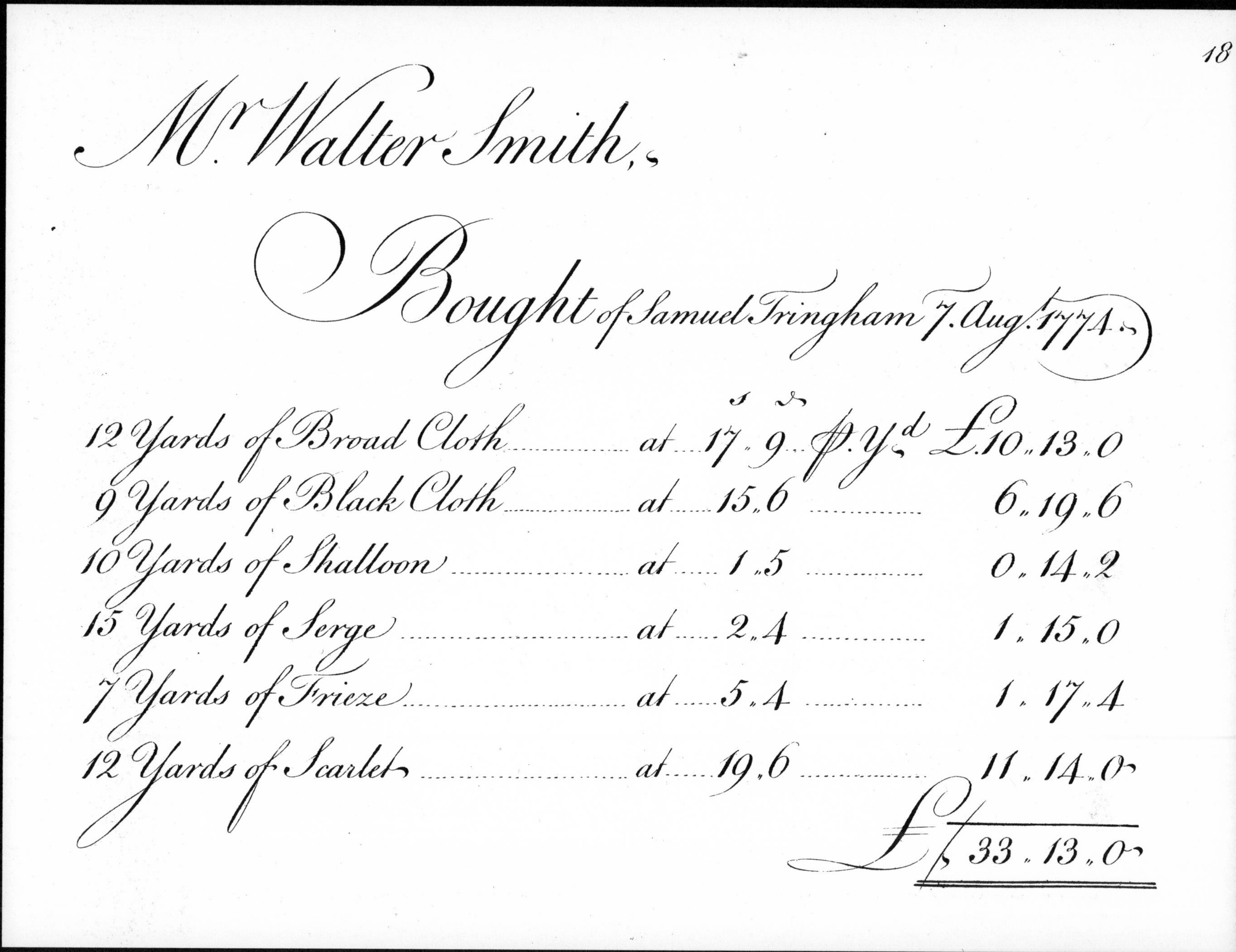

18

Mr Walter Smith,

Bought of Samuel Tringham 7. Aug. 1774

12 Yards of Broad Cloth	at	17 „ 9 ℗. Yᵈ	£ 10 „ 13 „ 0
9 Yards of Black Cloth	at	15 „ 6	6 „ 19 „ 6
10 Yards of Shalloon	at	1 „ 5	0 „ 14 „ 2
15 Yards of Serge	at	2 „ 4	1 „ 15 „ 0
7 Yards of Frieze	at	5 „ 4	1 „ 17 „ 4
12 Yards of Scarlet	at	19 „ 6	11 „ 14 „ 0
		£	33 „ 13 „ 0

Newington. 18. Septem.r 1774

19

Honoured Sir,

In Obedience to your Commands, I send this to inform you what Advances I have made in my Writing. I find now by Experience, that to write a bold free hand correctly requires no Small Care and Application: But this is no discouragement to me, since you have frequently told me that to write a good hand would be more serviceable to my Designs, than any other Learning, which if I attain I perswade myself you expect no more from

Honoured Sir,

Your dutiful Son

Ishmael Smart

73

Joseph Webb

Webb's Useful Penmanship. 1796

The title of this work – 'Webb's Useful Penmanship' – shows how far things have moved by the end of the century from 'The Pen-man's Paradis', with its gay flourishes and calligraphic monsters, at the beginning. The way ahead is equally plain, for the next century, with the spread of free education, would carry the plain rather monotonous style throughout the new schools.

$7\frac{1}{4} \times 11\frac{1}{4}$ inches

L 542–1939

Manuscript

Copy-book written by William Turner. 1834

The first page of a manuscript copy-book written out by William Turner, possibly when he was a pupil at Bray's Academy, Barnstaple.

9¼ × 14½ inches

L 3320–1965

Philosophy is then only va luable when it serves for the law of life, and not for the ostentation of science.

Manuscript

Copy-book written by William Turner. 1834

Another page from William Turner's copy book. On the original it is just possible to see the faint pencil lines, between which he wrote his copy.

$9\frac{1}{4} \times 14\frac{1}{2}$ inches

L 3320–1965

Manuscript

Copy-book written by William Turner. 1834

William Turner's exercise here shows one of the prevailing faults of this type of hand, in its insistence on excessive 'thicks' and 'thins', so that part of the letter disappears and the result is difficult to read.

$9\frac{1}{4} \times 14\frac{1}{2}$ inches

L 3320–1965

Deus creavit coelum et terram intra sex dies.
Deus creavit coelum et terram intra sex dies.
Deus creavit coelum et terram intra sex dies.
Deus creavit coelum et terram intra sex dies.
Deus creavit coelum et terram intra sex dies.
Deus creavit coelum et terram intra sex dies.
Deus creavit coelum et terram intra sex dies.
Deus creavit coelum et terram intra sex dies.
Deus creavit coelum et terram intra sex dies.
Deus creavit coelum et terram intra sex dies.
Deus creavit coelum et terram intra sex dies.

Edward Riches.

Manuscript

Copy-book written by Edward Riches.
(First half of 19th century)

In this example and the succeeding one, the teacher appears to have written the first line of the copy, and the pupil has continued it with varying success down the page. This form of instruction has been, and continues to be, familiar to most schoolchildren at some stage of learning.

9 × 14½ inches

L 3321–1965

78

Manuscript

Copy-book written by Edward Riches.
(First half of 19th century)

The somewhat shaky and uncertain efforts of the schoolboy contrast painfully with the copy-books of the masters we have been considering.

9 × 14½ inches

L 3321–1965

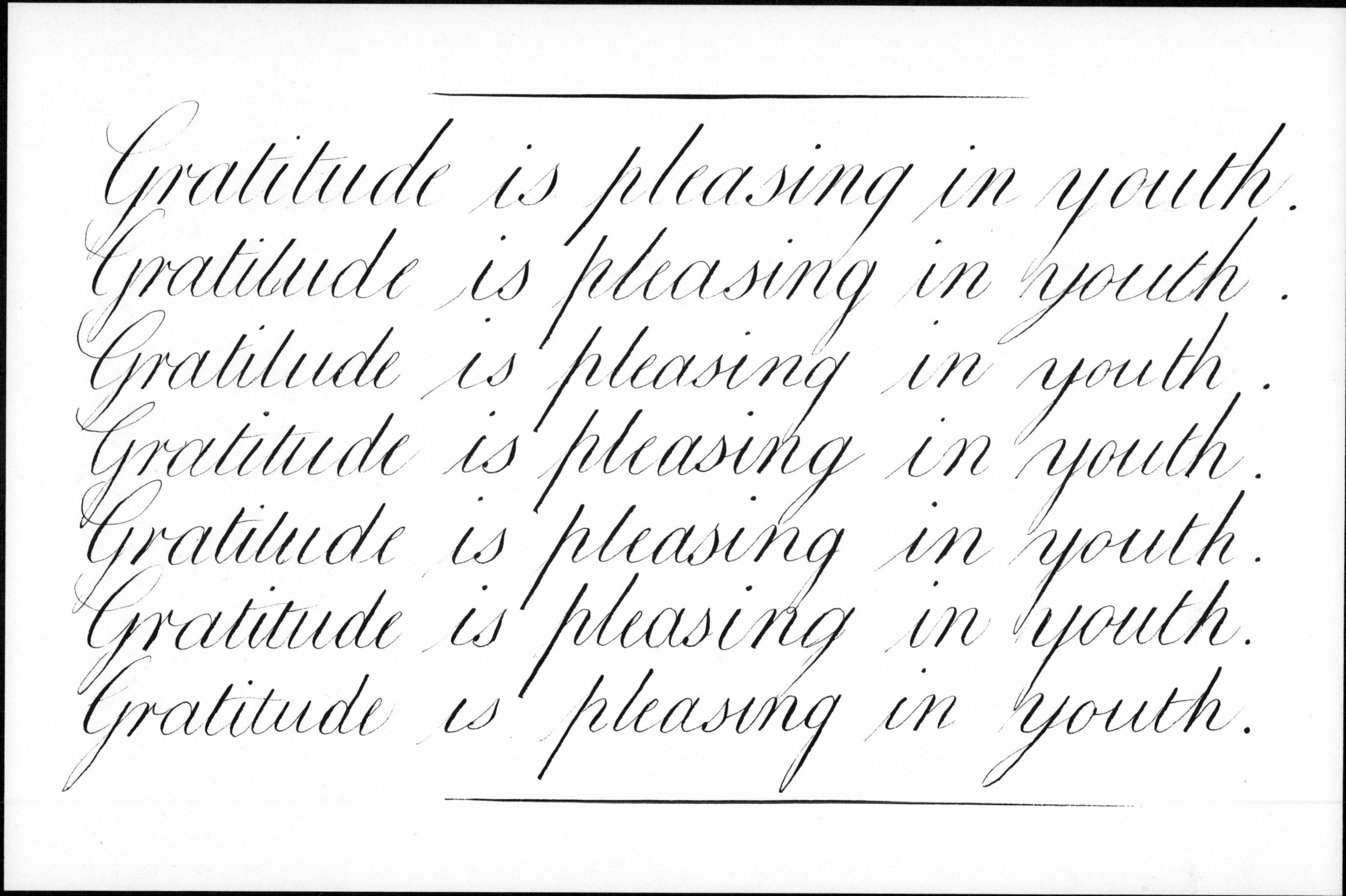

Gratitude is pleasing in youth.
Gratitude is pleasing in youth.
Gratitude is pleasing in youth.
Gratitude is pleasing in youth.
Gratitude is pleasing in youth.
Gratitude is pleasing in youth.
Gratitude is pleasing in youth.

Easingwold

Encourage all honest and virtuous actions.

Encouragement most commonly animates the mind.

Formentera

Fame most commonly accompanies merit.

Fear is commonly the companion of guilty actions.

79 and 80

Cassell and Co.

Cassell's Popular Educator, vol. II. 1853

These two examples from 'The Popular Educator' by Cassell and Co. fittingly close this survey of English handwriting, and together with Mulhauser's 'Manual of Writing' indicate the start of a new development. Writing was now to be taught to a far wider range of pupils, until education was universal and compulsory. But for those who were too old to benefit from the new era, the self-help manuals, such as this, would offer opportunity to improve themselves. For these people a few simple styles were all that need be taught or mastered.

$10\frac{3}{4} \times 7\frac{1}{2}$ inches

LESSONS IN PENMANSHIP. 69

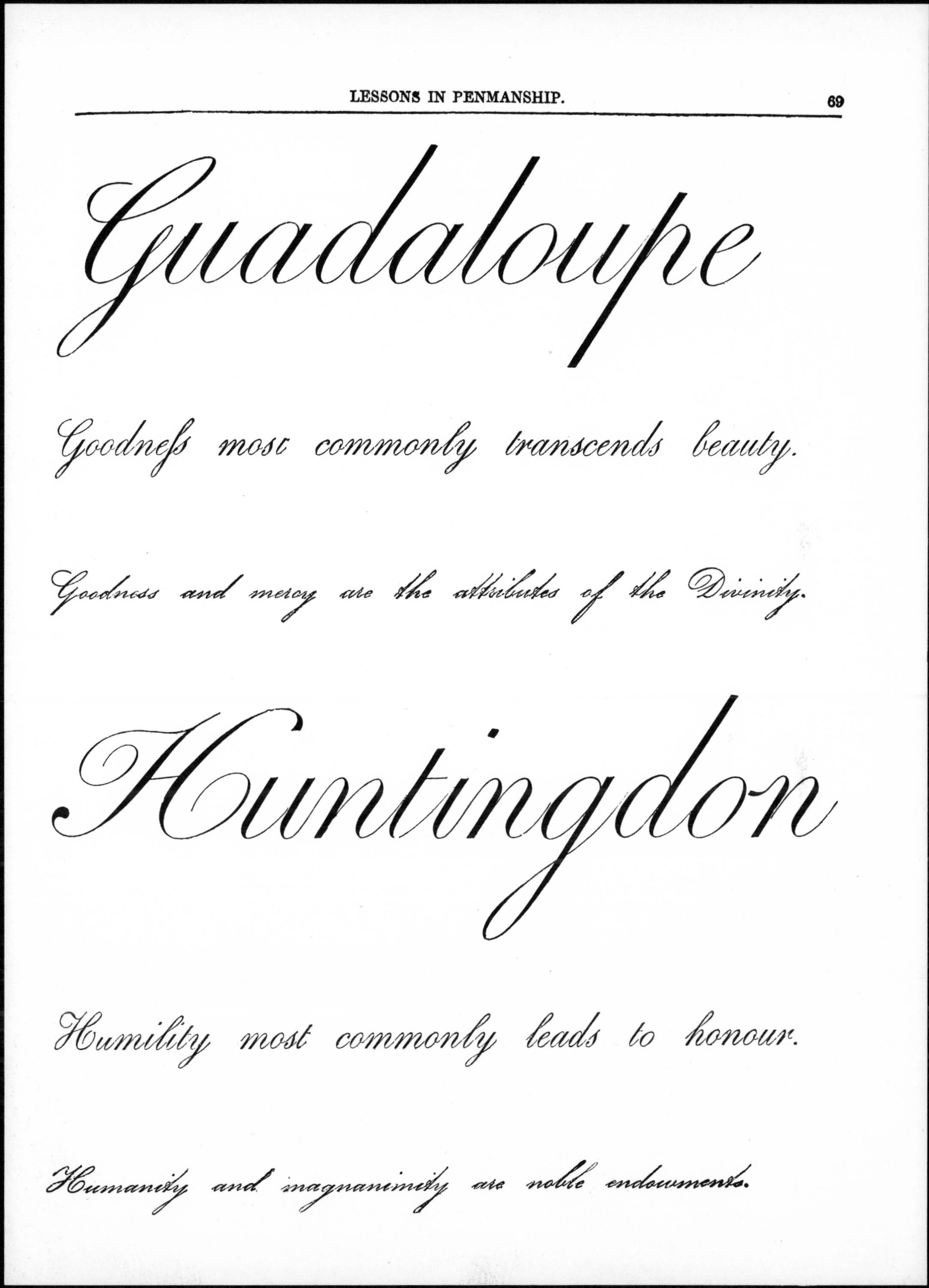

Guadaloupe

Goodneſs most commonly transcends beauty.

Goodness and mercy are the attributes of the Divinity.

Huntingdon

Humility most commonly leads to honour.

Humanity and magnanimity are noble endowments.

John Davies

The Writing Schoolemaster. 1648

*This illustration, taken from the 17th century
copy-book of John Davies, gives a pictorial illustration
of the method of holding the pen. This sort of instruction
or possibly a verbal one (plate 82), is to be found in most
copy-books. Two hundred years later we find a similar
illustration, this time showing the hand with a steel pen
(plate 89).*

L 3070–1960

How to hold the Pen.

TAke the Pen in your hand, and place your Thumb on that fide thereof
which is next your Breaft, not extending it fo low as the end of your
fore-finger ; next to that, place your fore-finger on the top of the Pen,
lower then your thumb about a quarter of an inch : Laftly, place your middle
finger fo much lower then that, on the further fide of the Pen. Let there be
very little fpace or diftance betwixt the Pen and your fore-finger, but let both
that and your middle finger be extended almoft to their full length : Obferve
alfo that your Thumb rife and fall in the joynt, as the length or compafs of
the Letters require which you write, and that your little finger onely reft on
the paper; nor let there be the leaft preffure of your hand, but bear it up with
an eafie pulfe.

How

How to manage and uʃe the Pen.

HAving a Book to write in, or a fheet of paper to write on, which muft
be ruled with lines with a black-lead Pen or a pair of Compaffes,
but they are beft ; for if the body of the Hand you write be deep, as
the Roman and Italian are, you may with them, being fet at a fit diftance,
rule your Lines double, and thereby every Letter will be kept even at head
and at foot. The want of Compaffes may be fupplied by a Quill cut forked,
which I take to be an inftrument of more certainty for that purpofe, your
paper lying in a good light on a Desk, or on fomething made floping (it being
not fo good to write on what is directly level) and ftreight before you, your
Elbow lying even with the midft of the end thereof ; your hand bending out-
ward or from you ; having before dipt onely the nib of your Pen into the
Ink with its hollow fide downward, then begin to imitate an Alphabet of the
hand you intend to write ; and when your eye is from your Copy you write
by, be fure it be juft at the end of your pen as you move it; and when you
make any part of a Letter confifting of a full downright ftroke, hold your
Pen right forward, turn not the nib thereof any way, but it lying flat, at

once

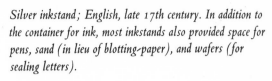

83

Silver inkstand; English, late 17th century. In addition to the container for ink, most inkstands also provided space for pens, sand (in lieu of blotting-paper), and wafers (for sealing letters).

$2 \times 7\frac{1}{2} \times 5\frac{1}{3}$ inches

M 579–1924

To make Ink.

TAke three Ounces of Galls which are small and heavy and crisp, put
them in a vessell of three pints of Wine, or of Rain-water, which is
much better, letting it stand so infusing in the Sun for one or two dayes;
Then take two Ounces of Coppris, or of Roman Vitrial, well colour'd and
beaten small, stirring it well with a stick, which being put in, set it again in the
Sun for one or two dayes more. Stir all together, adding two Ounces of Gum
Arabique of the clearest and most shining, being well beaten. And to make
your Ink shine and lustrous, add certain pieces of the Barque of Pomgranat,
or a small quantity of double-refin'd Sugar, boyling it a little over a gentle
fire. Lastly, pour it out, and keep it in a vessell of Glasse, or of Lead well
covered.

NOw its probable, what I intend as Medicine for the good of All, will be evil-
ly entertain'd, and converted into Poyson by some, (for this will appear
before faces sowre enough to turn Nectar into Vinegar, and those of our own
Faculty too) the reason whereof (though mainly for want of Reason) may be guest
at,

Come buy my fine Writing Ink!

Through many a street and many a
town
The Ink-man shapes his way;
The trusty Ass keeps plodding on,
His master to obey.

Directions for Learners

4

The proportion of Letters is regulated by the O & N; therefore practise them first in a large Character.

Make All Your Body-Strokes with the Full, & all Hair-Strokes with the corner of Your Pen.

Never turn Your Pen, nor alter the Position of Your hand.

Let Your hair-Strokes be proportion'd to Your Body-Strokes & answer one another.

Your Letters without Items must be even at top & bottom.

Let Your Items above be equal in length to l (t only excepted)

Your Items below must be equal in length to j.

Let Your Capitals be equal in height

85 *(left)*

Part of the 'Directions for Learners' from an 18th-century engraved copy-book (The Young Clerk's Assistant).

$8\frac{1}{2} \times 6$ inches

1550–1887

86 *(right)*

Silver inkstand by Paul de Lamerie; English, London hall-mark for 1729–30. On the tray stands an ink-well, a sand-box and a handbell to summon a servant.

$1\frac{1}{4} \times 8\frac{3}{4}$ inches

M155-C-1939

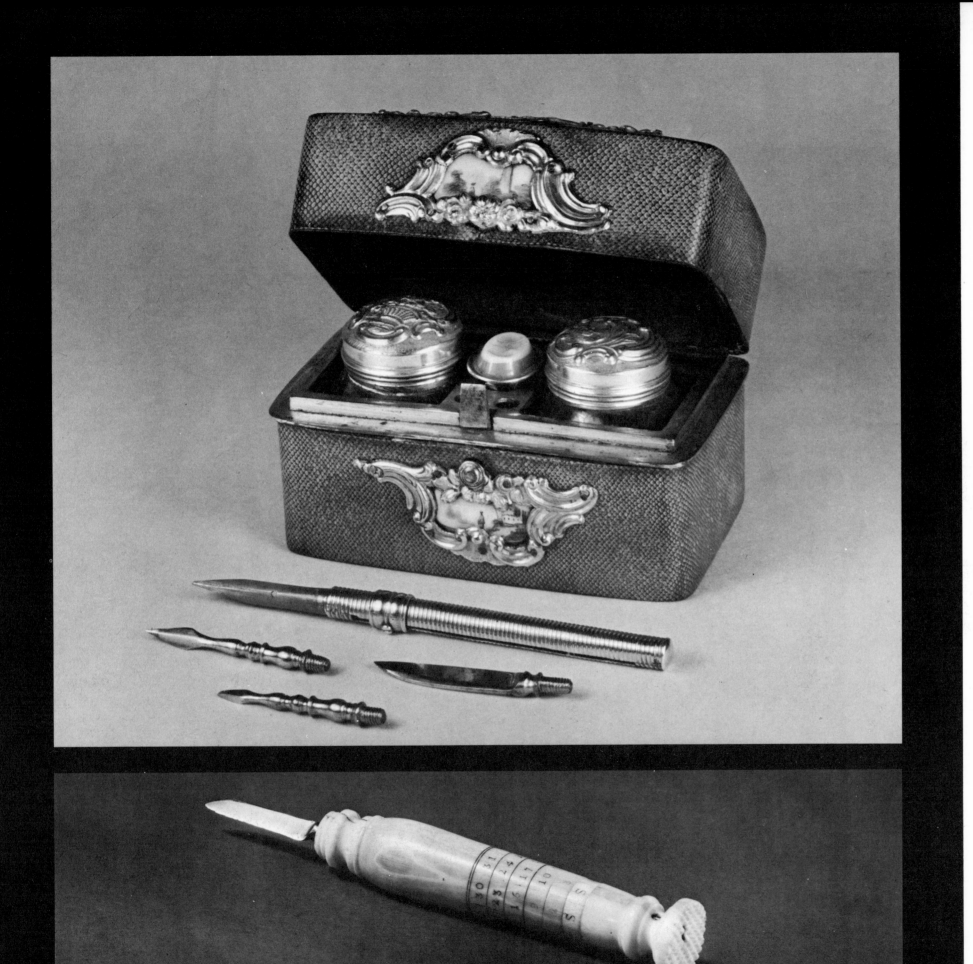

87a (above)

A small portable writing-box covered with shagreen and with painted enamel decoration in metal mounts. The various items displayed in front of the box can all be fitted inside it – one, a seal, has been left in its place between the lids of the two bottles, and holes for some of the other fitments can be seen in front of it. English, late 18th century.

$2 \times 3 \times 1\frac{3}{4}$ inches

C415-1914

87b (below)

An ivory pen-knife, for sharpening and making quill points. The blade can be fitted into the handle, which is engraved with a perpetual calendar. The opposite end could be impressed on sealing-wax. English, late 18th century. (In the possession of Mrs. Jill Robson.)

A porcelain inkstand in royal blue and gold, with a painted landscape decoration in the pen-trays. English (Derby), about 1820.

4 × 11¾ inches

C 1278–1919

finger, as seen in the figure of the hand, so that a thin paper-holder might pass a little way between this part of the pen and the knuckle. It is of essential importance to observe this part of the directions as well as the preceding, because for want of attention to these apparently trifling minutiæ, or small matters, many bad writers, or Cakographers, have arisen, and some of them even teachers who ought to know better what they are engaged in. For it stands to reason, and any one may prove it to himself by a few trials, that if the pen is allowed to fall below the knuckle, there is an instant loss of power, and of all real command over the pen.

Another direction of equal importance with any of those we have now given, is the position of the thumb; this you bend outwards from the pen so as to cause the tip or fleshy part of the point of the thumb to rest upon the pen directly opposite the

first joint of the forefinger, as shown in the figure of the hand. This completes the directions for the position of the *three* fingers which hold the pen. Now let us attend to the other two fingers. One of these, the little finger, must be held so as to touch the paper on which you intend to write, just on the tip of it close by the *side* of the nail, while the hand itself is made to rest upon its heel, that is, close by the wrist, not pressing heavily, but as lightly as possible. In fact,

if once you acquire a habit of leaning on the table or lolling upon it with your chest or stomach you need never expect to be a Calligrapher. We believe that many pupils have been seriously injured in their health by the practice or habit of leaning upon the chest while learning to write, and that such injury has followed them through life. What can be more absurd than to see a boy or girl sprawling on a table or desk with their arms akimbo, and their noses almost upon the paper imitating the motion of the pen? What more foolish or disagreeable than to see every stroke of the pen imitated by the mouth or the tongue, as if the writer was approaching a state of idiocy? Let every student of penmanship sit erect like a lady or gentleman while writing, and let him only stoop his head with a gentle inclination, as we said before, sufficient to enable him to see clearly what he is doing, and to

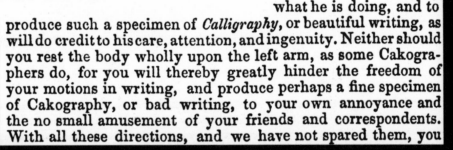

METHOD OF HOLDING THE PEN.

produce such a specimen of *Calligraphy*, or beautiful writing, as will do credit to his care, attention, and ingenuity. Neither should you rest the body wholly upon the left arm, as some Cakographers do, for you will thereby greatly hinder the freedom of your motions in writing, and produce perhaps a fine specimen of Cakography, or bad writing, to your own annoyance and the no small amusement of your friends and correspondents. With all these directions, and we have not spared them, you

89

Cassell and Co.

Cassell's Popular Educator, vol. II. 1853

Over a period of three hundred years the writing-books continued to give instruction on how to sit, how to place the paper and how to hold the pen. 'What more foolish or disagreeable' asks the 'Popular Educator,' 'than to see every stroke of the pen imitated by the mouth or the tongue, as if the writer was approaching a state of idiocy? Let every student of penmanship sit erect like a lady or gentleman, and let him only stoop his head with a gentle inclination.' And this useful journal continues to explain in great detail exactly how the fingers should be placed in relation to the pen, just as its predecessors had done from the beginning.

$10\frac{3}{4} \times 7\frac{1}{2}$ inches

M. A. Mulhauser

A Manual of Writing founded on Mulhauser's
Method of Teaching Writing and Adapted to
English Use. 1844

*Although this illustration of a writing class appears in a book
of the mid-19th century, there can be no doubt that it
represents a scene familiar over many years. Since it appears
in the book laid down as the manual for teaching writing in
the schools under the Committee of the Council on
Education, it also stands at the beginning of the new era of
mass education.*

(By permission of the Librarian, University of London Library.)

GLOSSARY OF HANDS

a b c d e f g h i k l m n o p q r ſ t u x. y z et ſt w &.

SECRETARY HAND: 1571

A A O G Q T S C E F J ff

N N M V W V P P R B B

B D D I L K H H X Y Z Z

a b c d œ e f f g h i k ll m n o p q r r ſt s t v u w x y z

SECRETARY HAND: 1637

A a b c d d e e e f f g h i k l ll m n o p q r ſs ſt t v u w x yz et

ENGROSSING SECRETARY
HAND: 1658

A B C D E F ff G H J K L M N O P P

Q R S T V U W W X Y Z A B C D E F

A a b c d e e e f g h t h i k l m n o p p q r r ſs s t v u w x y z et

SLOPED SECRETARY
HAND: 1663
(but written much earlier)

A a b c c d d e e f f g h h h i ij k k l all m n

N n o p p q q r r s ſs s t v u w x y y z z t

MIXED HANDS
(Round-hand): c.1670

A a b c c d d e f g g h i k l m n o p q r s t v u w x y z

From *The later court hands in England from the fifteenth to the seventeenth century*, by Hilary Jenkinson, Cambridge, 1927.
(By permission of the Cambridge University Press.)